The Silent Killer Below

Hunting and Healing Geopathic Stress

Robert Egby

A Dowser's Notebook

The Silent Killer Below

Hunting and Healing Geopathic Stress

Robert Egby

Author of the Award Winning Books:
The Quest of the Radical Spiritualist
INSIGHTS: The Healing Paths of the Radical Spiritualist
HOLY DIRT, SACRED EARTH a Dowser's Journey in New Mexico

Three Mile Point Publishing
Pemberton, New Jersey

Published by:
Three Mile Point Publishing
13 Wynwood Drive
Pemberton, NJ 08068 USA
www.robertegbybooks.com
Phone: 1- 609-351-5878

Book formatting and cover design: Jera Publishing

Back cover image shows a row of trees flanking a park in Springfield Township, NJ. A cluster of geopathic stress zones created malformed trees that eventually died. The zones have since been cleared by the Author.

First published
Three Mile Point Publishing
November 2018

ISBN: 978-0-9848664-8-9

Library of Congress Control Number: 2018956993

Printed in the United States of America

DEDICATION

This book is dedicated to my friend and mentor the late Tom Passey, Canadian Dowser Extraordinaire who said:

> *"Dowsing is the finding and decreeing is the order to the Cosmos for an action to be carried out. It's the same as ask and you shall receive. How many times does one have to be told?"*

To my wonderful partner and dowsing companion Betty Lou Kishler who is never afraid to beat on doors and ask questions.

To all the people who suffered from geopathic stress and made this book possible by sharing their stories, my heartfelt thanks and appreciation.

To all the people who suffered and said: "If only I had known…" give this book to a friend whose husband is suffering yet stubbornly fails to believe.

And to Google Earth—the Eye in the sky— which made many parts of this book possible.

Love, Light and Blessings.
Robert
Pemberton, NJ

CONTENTS

INTRODUCTION

Hello, many years ago when as a journalist and news photographer I trod the sidewalks of Nicosia in British Colonial Cyprus with Lawrence Durrell (author of The Alexandria Quartet), I ventured to ask his secret for writing a best-selling book. "Grade six!" he retorted. "Write for grade six and everybody will understand you."

Larry was public relations director at the time for the British authorities but I took his words seriously, in fact ever since in all my books I have made that my aim. In other words, this book "The Silent Killer Below" can be read and absorbed by just about everybody.

It is vital that people in all walks of life should understand the gravity of the geopathic stress situation in the United States, not simply because of the unnecessary suffering and needless destruction of families, but the flagrant wall of deliberate ignorance that exists from the Administration in Washington, D.C. to the community leaders around us. Mention the words "Geopathic Stress" to a realtor, an architect, a construction engineer, even a journalist and he or she will either shrug and walk on — some may even run away as a realtor did with us.

And so, welcome to my notebook. For starters, it does not have the structure of a normal textbook. It is, to all intents and purposes, a Notebook of things happening in Energy, our domiciles, but more importantly — we the people living in the battle zones.

The information in this book may enlighten, intrigue or downright annoy you. It may also enable you and your loved ones to live a healthier life because it is also an instruction book — a DIY.

Robert Egby
Pemberton, New Jersey
October 2018

1

GOOGLE EARTH: OUR EYE IN THE SKY

When I was young in England, those years before the Second World War when cart-horses pulled hay wagons, the larks sang high in the blue heavens and a bar of Cadbury chocolate sold for a penny, I never dreamed of things like dowsing rods and pendulums that could track energies, water and mysterious stuff like that. If I had told my mother that one day I would look down on Earth and houses and make drawings of where good and bad energies exist, she would either have hustled me off to the local psychologist or simply flaked over in a faint.

The nearest telephone, a call-box outside a confection and tobacco store was at least a half mile away and she would never use that: "too modern." When in 1969 she died of cancer that hid within an arthritic spine it took me a lot of years to finally discover she spent her last days unable to stand up and agonizing on a geopathic stress zone — the Silent Killer!

In my grief I thought: "If only I had known."

If there is any higher learning from what technology affords us, it is contained in the words: it is dangerous to be ignorant of the world in which we live. Thus in case you are not up to speed, let us take a few lines to tell you what made this book possible in the field of dowsing.

The technology is known on this planet as Google Earth and Christopher Columbus would have loved it.

If you have yet to discover it, Google Earth is a computer program that renders a 3D representation of Earth based on satellite imagery — an eye in the sky. The program comprehensively maps the Earth by the superimposition of images obtained from satellites, aerial photography and GIS (Geographic Information System) data onto a three-dimensional globe. This permits users to view any landscape, city, village and street on Earth. A woman once complained that Google Earth invaded her privacy by showing her cat sitting on the doorstep of her New York home.

When a person first uses it, he or she may get a feeling of playing god, but that soon goes. For dowsers armed with magnifiers scanning expensive charts or maps of countries, town and village landscapes it offers a new dimension in map reading. So much so, that energy lines anywhere in the world can be dowsed to within an accuracy of one or two feet and certainly less than a meter.

When tracking down ley lines in Egypt, the Middle East, Europe and across North America for our book "Chasing the Cosmic Principle," Google Earth Pro was the software that made it possible. Dowsing this way we tracked the William Penn Ley that runs all along North and South Broad Streets for many miles and includes Philadelphia's spectacular City Hall. The accuracy was plus or minus one foot.

For this book, a dowser specializing in digital map dowsing and energy transmutation can, by using Google Earth, track and neutralize a geopathic stress zone in a house or office in a neighboring town or even a home or a farm in Australia — almost 12,000 miles away on the other side of the planet. Transmutation? That's a high-brow name for healing or simply neutralizing or moving natural energy.

If you think all this borders on the miraculous or mind-blowing, the change in energy status is not "perhaps it will happen" or perhaps tardy, it happens instantly, seemingly faster than the speeds of light and thought. It is stunning and what is more the change can be made permanent.

How to successfully perform healing or neutralization of distant negative energies is explained later in this book. How it happens exactly is still a mystery but some investigative experts are working on this.

If you plan on being a cyber dowser download Google Earth Pro — it is free — and learn to use it. It is loaded with gadgets such as taking leaves off trees so you can clearly see a building to adding yellow pins to mark leys, geopsirals and particularly for this book, geopathic stress zones.

You need to learn how to save a map containing your dowsing scan as JPEG. This is a compression system, critically useful in your communications. Most of the photos on your laptop will probably be saved as JPEG. Once you know how to use Google Earth, it is a very easy and extremely useful tool. You will see how easy it is to scan the railway station on Ulitsa Russkaya, Vladivostok, Russia as it is Aunt Mary's place across the street. It is a good investment to spend time "playing around" and learning the system. Practice while reading this book. It pays off well.

2

IGNORANCE AT LARGE: "IF ONLY I HAD KNOWN"

It is a nasty side of America of which the majority are unaware. Millions endure sleepless nights, their bodies wracked in unexplainable pains and discomforts. It's a life where pain-killers, opiods, narcotics are the main meals of the day. Doctor visits, optimistic for a solution, always flop. The duties of life—raising the kids, enjoying life with loved ones and friends—are now distant memories. The dream houses they bought a few short years ago are now unexplainable hell-holes and no one seems to have answers.

No one wants to look under the beds of Americans and say: "You have a health problem." Even when a family becomes totally dysfunctional and "foreclosure" looms on the approaching horizon, no one wants to know about geopathic stress zones. Yet one brief survey in this book suggests all foreclosed homes in America suffer from toxic Earth energy. It is called geopathic stress zones or "GSZ".

This book started as a workshop handout to help people clear so called "sick" houses and resume normal lives. It developed into a flag warning that cultural blindness is costing the United States not only long lasting pain and discomfort in the homes, but multi-billions of dollars in health care could be saved if minds were open and educated. This applies particularly to men where for some strange reason, ignorance reigns supreme even to the point of death as we shall hear.

Of the 170 homes cleared of toxic energy during the research and writing of this book only four were requested by men. The rest were pleas from women who frequently confided: "I haven't told my husband. I'm waiting to see how his health improves."

This book tells how geopathic stress zones can be found easily using human in-born intuition and how it can be neutralized using either a simple physical bar or an even cleaner way, by mental decree. If these methods were taught in high schools and junior colleges across the country, that small effort would save an unimaginable amount of agony and lives plus billions of dollars in health costs.

The saddest quote that dowsers hear at various times, hits hard. It is the widow who looks at the bed where her husband died and says: "If only I had known." That is society's blunder!

We often read newspaper columnists decrying dowsing as a "pseudo science", "unprovable", "hokey" and even "fraudulent." Dowsing, divination or whatever you choose to call the practice is not a science, it is closer to an art form in that each action, each divination, each dowse is unique, a demonstration of higher consciousness at work.

Dowsing, divination and radiesthesia are ancient skills recorded in the Bible, written on clay tablets by the Sumerians, the stones and monuments of the Egyptians and the Greeks, plus the ancient scrolls of India and China. The Art of Dowsing was totally suppressed for centuries in what is known as the "Dark Ages" by the Roman Universal Catholic Church. The shadows of that period still haunt and linger in the minds of today's journalists, scientists and indeed many ordinary home bodies who claim to live with open minds.

"If only I had known" is an acknowledgement that humanity has failed in its desire to be like the Cosmic force — the Creator, the Source of its Being, Infinite Intelligence, Holy Spirit, God or whoever you believe is the guiding force of the Cosmos.

A PLEA FROM WANDA

The email popped up silently on Google mail. It was a simple plea to "check our home for geopathic stress zones." Then an address, plain and simple. No indication of what was to come.

A Google Earth chart with dowsed yellow lines was emailed back. "Dear W. Yes, you do have a problem with two distinct geopathic stress zones (GSZ) running through the home. Both are subterranean water veins, a few inches wide with water running over broken rock and clay plus minerals. The GSZ AA is about 110 feet down, the other GSZ BB is about 70 feet down. Both run North-east and both are permanent, in other words not seasonal. How long have you lived here and what have been the problems? Also there is a third zone crossing the entrance to the driveway. Was there a tree standing there, probably bent and twisted? Anyway, a GSZ crossing the driveway can deter visitors or people coming in. Zones on the driveway are bad when trying to sell places. People are hesitant in coming to look. Use the yellow lines on the picture to see how they have affected you and the family. We need your permission to clear."

Wanda replied: "We have lived here for 15 years. We built the house ourselves, my husband is in construction. My son B has autism. He had it before we moved here, he was six. My daughter has social anxiety, a line goes through her bedroom. Though she lives in New York now she still as problems with it. I have stomach problems, fatigue problems, sometimes sleeping problems, and inflammation, extreme food sensitivities. I work with J (a therapist) who has helped me greatly. I exercise regularly and eat perfectly."

"Since we have moved here our marriage has deteriorated, I always thought it was due to the stress of autism. I spend all my energy making B the best autistic person he can be, which also takes a lot of money. We are near farms. The property here was once used as a dumping grounds as glass and metal come out of the ground around us. The driveway situation is interesting. We rarely have friends over and even though I'm very social something always stops me! If you have any questions let me know, I'm an open book. If you can do the clearing tomorrow it would be great!"

It was such a heart crying for help that we cleared the property within the hour, much the same as dowsers do remote map readings and remote healing — except this was a well designed upscale house in Hunterdon County outside a scenic village 40 miles away from our base in Pemberton, New Jersey. The next morning Wanda replied: "My husband has had the best night's sleep for years."

This is the most rewarding comment that dowsers can hear. It's like music to their ears. Even before the current high-tech remote dowsing era dowsers were familiar with two familiar echoes: "Why didn't somebody tell us about this?" and "There are monsters under our beds and they are being ignored."

Geopathic stress zones can prevail anywhere. You may have a posh or swanky mansion in Florida or Washington State, or your property might be a shack on skid row or any place in between, there is a good chance there's a geopathic stress zone working silently in one of the rooms. They can lurk unknown and unseen in an office, store, school, college or even your home. In addition, as we shall see there is scientific evidence that they lurk on roads and highways, in fact some of the high-ratio accident intersections in North America are riddled with geopathic stress zones.

Here's a conundrum: Geopathic stress does not directly injure or kill people. It works silently and indirectly by simply reducing our human defenses — the immune system. On a highway it is said to cause "momentary loss of consciousness."

WHAT IS GEOPATHIC STRESS EXACTLY?

Earth energy is totally sublime. We are so used to it most people are not even aware of it. Those who do, may personify it as Gaia life force because it is here and all around us. Gaia is an attractive hypothesis because it is named after the Greek Earth goddess, Gaia. The theory was created in the 1960s by a NASA scientist Dr James Lovelock who was looking at methods of detecting life on Mars. One could easily suggest Earth energy is a beautiful and invisible aura that enshrouds us on a rock that's hurtling through space at 67,000 miles an hour. Generally it does that quite well without leaving a ripple in our coffee or beer.

Geophysicists are reasonably sure that the Earth has a magnetic field because it oscillates at an average frequency of 7.83 Hz or Hertz which almost matches the range of human brainwaves, particularly the alpha mode which is the relaxing, light meditative or creative state in the human body.

The German physicist Winfried Schumann identified this frequency in 1952 and it became known as "brain waves" or the Schumann Resonance. Schumann discovered that these waves create a virtual match between Earth radiation and human consciousness. When the mind and body are attuned to 7.83 Hz, humanity's whole being functions beautifully and stays healthy.

Scientists have suggested that these waves influence the body's biological clock. During hours of darkness the waves reduce in intensity and encourage sleep and restoration. If you follow the power of numbers you will recognize that 7.83 Hz reduces to nine — the Cosmic Nine!

Having trouble in believing the Earth's electromagnetic field exists? ScienceDaily.com reports how Pauline Fleischmann and Robin Grob, researchers at the Biocentre of the University of Würzburg have studied Desert Ants which use the Earth's energy field to get back home.

The news item reports: "Before an ant sets out to forage, it has to calibrate its navigational system. For this purpose, the insects exhibit a rather peculiar behavior during two to three days: They perform so-called learning walks to explore the vicinity of the nest entrance and frequently turn about their vertical body axes while doing so.

"High-speed video recordings show that the ants stop repeatedly during these pirouetting motions. What is special about the longest of these stopping phases is that at this moment the ants always look back precisely to the nest entrance, although they are unable to see the tiny hole in the ground. Researchers have now made the surprising discovery that the Desert Ant uses the Earth's magnetic field as an orientation cue during these calibration trips. This ability had been previously unknown for desert ants." This textual illustration shows that even Desert Ants can dowse.

The center of the Earth, the core, has two parts. The solid inner core is composed of iron which is surrounded by a liquid outer core composed of a nickel-iron alloy. The inner core spins at a different speed than the rest of the planet. This, according to NASA geologists is thought to cause Earth's magnetic field. It's a natural dynamo! (See PHOTOS #1 on page 107.)

One group of scientists and engineers at the Saitribai Phule Pune University in India put it this way: "The earth is one gigantic magnet and it generates a massive energy field that is constantly fluctuating." It is so soft, silent and a part of us, we take it for granted. Some people figure it does not even exist until one day, they suddenly realize they have been living in something called geopathic stress. And that too is soft and silent but toxic and deadly.

This happens when the Earth's beneficial electromagnetic field becomes distorted. This distortion causes stress not just within our human bodies but in all living things, pets, animals, birds, vegetation and trees. Trees are the hardest hit because they cannot walk or fly away.

GENTLE, SOFT AND DEADLY

The word Geopathic is derived from two Greek words: geo means 'of the earth', and pathos means 'suffering' or 'disease'. The word 'geopathic' literally means suffering or disease of the earth. Thus geopathic stress is the general term for energies radiating from the earth that cause discomfort and ill health in human beings. Because of their detrimental effect, they are often known as negative earth energies or simply toxic rays.

Over the years various dowsers and cultures have listed them as black streams, cancer rays, negative green rays, Hartmann and Curry grid lines and even negative ley lines. Feng Sui practitioners refer to the rays as Sha. Today, dowsers and others prefer to call them by the one name: geopathic stress. Another is a zone of disturbance. For this book the name is geopathic stress zone.

The question is how does this beautiful, beneficial energy become distorted?

The outer mantle of the planet is laced with streams of water. They resemble blood veins in the human body, they roam and flow, never in straight lines, more like a country stream roaming at will through the valleys of forests and meadows. When a water vein, often a few inches to a couple of feet wide, flows over clay, broken rock, geological fault lines, fissures, leachable rocks, the gentle Earth energy goes through a 180 degree phase change: it turns negative. Not only that, it continues to beam up to the Earth's surface and affects any living creature spending prolonged periods living or sleeping on these rays.

One of the fascinating aspects of geopathic stress is that it knows no barriers. Its energies pass through stone, tar, concrete, wood, walls, floors, rooftops, as if they did not exist. Windows, doors, furniture, beds, mattresses, do not hamper the rays. A fourteen inch wide geopathic energy zone in a basement is still 14 inches wide and just as powerful at a skyscraper's top floor one hundred levels up.

It is so extremely gentle and incredibly obscure that people have to live on a geopathic stress zone for weeks and months before its presence is felt. Even then, many people refuse to believe it exists, even when their bodies are wracked with pain from surgical operations, continual cramps, persistent headaches and other chronic afflictions. Men and women, ignorant of geopathic stress, frequently attribute their plights to normal everyday routine situations.

The popular excuses are age, excessive and stressful work, too much exercise or weight-lifting, over eating, insufficient sleep, lack of love and attention, penalties for leaving the church, not giving money to charities or "fooling around" with members of the opposite sex. Yes, as one man suffering from intestinal cancer said: "God is getting back at me for sleeping with another woman." The excuses are endless and sometimes creatively odd, such as: "I had a dream I was abducted by aliens and that's what started all this evil."

As we shall see, even when the family becomes totally dysfunctional and their home has been foreclosed, the last thing victims ever consider is the Silent Killer Below the bed, the armchair or the office seat.

Did we say geopathic stress knows no barriers? There is one and it's the enemy of many environmentalists — a sheet of plastic! Plastic is a natural energy blocker, but more on that later.

UNDERMINING THE IMMUNE SYSTEM

Another important and critical point: Geopathic stress is not directly responsible for any illness. What occurs from prolonged exposure is a reduction in the effectiveness of the immune system and this applies to humans, pets, farm animals, vegetables, bushes and trees. When the immune system becomes ineffective and dysfunctional it leaves the victim open to any sickness, but sadly cancer ranks high on the list of probables.

For various reasons, notably science, culture, religion and inbred skepticism, most Americans, particularly the male species have little or no knowledge of geopathic stress and countless — yes! - millions are suffering from the effects of this phenomenon and as you will see, responsible people in high places actually run away or totally ignore the problem.

Their main argument is this: Dowsing lacks scientific proof. American scientists are trained to accept only a phenomenon that can be repeated and statistically monitored and reported. It's time American scientists got out of their boxes and commence conducting tests as other scientists have been doing in Europe, India and Russia as we shall show.

Right now, let's talk about the gentle Art of Dowsing.

THE BASICS OF DOWSING

Most people do not usually associate dowsing with health and healing: they simply associate it with the search for water and minerals. This association perpetuates humanity's inability to defend itself, improve health and open up the doors to higher consciousness. This association, really a human limitation, actually condemns untold numbers of people to prolonged suffering and for some, death. This will become obvious as our journey progresses.

Right now, back to stage one.

Dowsing is a human faculty of using the higher consciousness to obtain information that would not normally be available to the conscious mind.

While some dowsers like to rely on sight and powers of intuition, some dowsers use only their higher consciousness to see and find information.

Currently, the traditional ways of dowsing a geopathic stress zone is with the use of L-rods so named because they are shaped like the capital letter L. Some dowsers still use traditional Y-shaped branches made from flexible trees such as the Willow.

L-rods come in all shapes and sizes from mini-two and three inch ones to 17-inch affairs. The only problem with the long ones comes when working outdoors and a strong breeze perks up. Some rods come in chrome and bronze plating and I have actually seen one, fur-lined with ribbons.

Then there are the do-it-yourself rods. All one needs is a metal coat hanger: cut off the hook section, measure off half way along the lower bar section, then cut it with a pair of pliers or wire cutters. At this point you have two potential L-rods. Bend them into 90 degree shapes, find some straws or the housing of an empty ball-point pen and you have handles.

The other critical dowsing tool is the pendulum, a small weight suspended on a short line made of string or chain. Some dowsers possess ostentatious ones decorated with gems or crystals, others have simple ones such as a half inch metal nut tied on a bootlace. Most dowsers pick whatever suits their personality and psyche.

How do you find a pendulum that suits your needs? Find a collection or a store with an ample supply and use a pendulum to point out "which one is good for me now?"

When performing remote dowsing or map reading on Google Earth I use a polished bronze tag and chain from an old electric light stand. It is unique and never moves from my desk. It sits in an old relic of the smoking age — an ash tray. Whatever pendulum you choose, keep it clean by placing it in a pouch and in this way it will avoid becoming contaminated with other energies.

You know of course that a pendulum has basically four responses to questions. YES, NO, CANNOT SAY, DO NOT KNOW. The pendulum can swing four ways: Clockwise, counter-clockwise, forwards and sideways. Once you know the response signals, the pendulum operator is usually set for life.

Some dowsers use their fingers for a phenomenon known as "deviceless dowsing". Hold the tips of your thumb and forefinger together and rub them gently. Feel the skin rubbing skin. Now, say to your higher self or higher consciousness: "When I ask a question and the answer is YES, show me a YES." Note how the rubbing feels. Once you have that, do exactly the same for NO, and note the difference. Deviceless dowsing is great for places where you wish to operate incognito without your dowser's hat.

Other dowsers, particularly energy hunters use their bodies to designate a negative or toxic zone. When you have been chasing such phenomena as geopathic stress and other toxic energies your body gets the "feel" of it: your feet feel heavy or "funny."

Another dowsing instrument that costs nothing but requires some practice is the Mind Pendulum. All you have to do is imagine a pendulum suspended in front of your eyes. It appears by request and you can make it as ornate or puritanical as you like. Simply ask it to show you the usual responses — yes, no, cannot say, do not know. Once you are set up: your Mind Pendulum is ready for use anywhere, any time. To be completely effective, you need to practice! — practice! — practice!

My old mentor and partner Tom Passey for many workshops in British Columbia and Washington State used to drill that into every student he met: "If you want to be a good pianist — practice. If you want to be a good tennis player — practice. If you wish to be a great mountaineer — practice. If you wish to be a good dowser — practice, practice, practice!" I still hear his voice today. A great and beloved dowser.

3

RECOGNIZING GEOPATHIC STRESS

There are people who remember as a small child they sobbed and screamed at parents that a monster was lurking under the bed, or perhaps hiding in the closet or in a worse case — "there's something with me in bed." Of course, to the traditional adult minds of Mom and Dad there was nothing there. "He's just having a bad dream," a parent might say to the other.

Poor kid! He climbed out of bed and slept on the floor in the corner, or found solace in another part of the house, perhaps on the sofa downstairs — and fell asleep. Anything to get away from that "something" in the bedroom that no one believes exists.

This scenario is played out regularly by small children. Babies have been known to crawl to the bottom of the cradle to escape the "something" that bothers them. Some babies, unable to move, have simply expired in what is termed SID — Sudden Infant Death Syndrome. This is described later in detail.

Children are quickly sensitive to the geopathic stress zones while many adults react more slowly, sometimes waiting for six months or even a year before yielding to unexplained body aches and occasional cramps.

Many adults are totally unconscious of what is happening in their homes, even when they glibly acknowledge that "something weird" is happening. How many people have said: "I don't sleep well. I wake up with sweats, my heart beating, and my body full of pain," yet when you ask how they survived when they spent some time away from the house most will exclaim "Great! No problem."

This begs the question: Are people so out of tune, unconscious of their home settings, they fear to consider the possibility there is something critically wrong with Earth energy under their home?

One afflicted homeowner said bluntly: "My home is my castle, it never dawned on me there could be a problem in the earth under my bed."

Even adults who frequently feel discomforts, rapid heart beats, sweating and inability to sleep while in bed, seek peace on a downstairs sofa, and quickly blame such sleep discomforts as "part of getting old," or the various aspects of work or daily living, travel, financial concerns, even relationships for their physical and mental problems.

One father of three children, suffering from acute intestinal pains said: "I can understand why my kids hate going to bed. My own bed is a monster." When the negative Earth energy was cleared from his home, he said: "Unbelievable! I've had the best night's sleep in years."

The monster in the bedroom was a Geopathic Stress Zone. It is not a fast acting process. You may live and sleep on one for months, even years before it starts to have a serious effect. The general consensus among health professionals aware of the phenomenon is that in many cases it appears to reduce the immune system and expose victims to physical ailments to which they are most prone.

Sensitives may realize a geopathic stress zone simply by spending a few minutes on site. Canadian Quester Tom Passey would become nauseous when standing on a zone. My partner Betty Lou becomes dizzy and when

I stand on one, my feet and legs feel heavy as lead. Dizziness or vertigo often happens when there is a geopathic stress zone present in the house.

"A STRESSED OUT LIFE!"

We live in a fast moving, high tech world while geopathic stress is not only silent and stealthy, it works slowly and generally unnoticed. For most people it may take months or even a year or two before they realize something is critically wrong under their beds — sometimes in fact their entire home. (See PHOTOS #2 on page 108.)

The geopathic stress zone (GSZ) impacts not just bedrooms. A realtor who came for hypnotherapy because of what she called "a stressed out life" revealed a tragic record of events in her second floor luxury apartment. Dowsing showed the GSZ route coming in through a corner balcony, through the lower level of her bed, under the chair where she ate meals, under the chair where she worked at real estate on her computer, and finally under the armchair used to watch television in the evenings.

It started when she had been in the apartment about ten months. A year was spent on pain killers, magnesium sprays and various medical tests. The second and third years were spent recovering from three surgical operations on her legs and complete loss of cartilage in her knees. The fourth year she stayed at home until one day a taxi-driver helped her into my office. A quick visit to her home set breaker rods placed in the corners of the apartment. This brought instant relief.

"Why on earth didn't somebody tell me about this years ago?" she cried. "I'm going to write to the newspapers." Sure to her word, she did but the letter was not published. A dangerous phenomenon that nobody including editors and realtors do not wish to know and she was a realtor!

Every year some two million households are constructed in the United States. How many sites were checked and cleared by dowsers? Probably an infinitesimal number. Some skeptics will quickly jeer at such as question and continue to bathe in the mud of ignorance. Yet in Europe there are towns and communities where this actually happens: Dowsers accompanied by engineers actually check for toxic energy zones and clear them before building a housing complex, apartments and yes — schools. This is not just some recent 21st century environmental kick, it is a practice that is nearly a century old since a scientist/dowser discovered that over 5,000 people in one town died from cancer because they slept on geopathic stress zones — toxic energy coming from below the Earth's surface.

EARLY SIGNS OF GEOPATHIC STRESS

Because people spend a considerable amount of time in bed — six to nine hours a night — and sleep in one general area, it is probably the epitome of wisdom to be aware of the symptoms that can arise through the presence of zones of disturbance.

1. Refusal to go to bed. "I'd rather sleep on the sofa."
2. Opposition to going to bed. A person pleads insomnia.
3. Restlessness. Unable to fall asleep for hours.
4. Nightmares.
5. Feelings of a "presence" in the bed. This occurs mainly with young children.
6. Children insist a monster or ghost lurks in the closet or under the bed.
7. An aversion to certain spots in the bed.
8. A feeling of "falling out" of bed.
9. Sleepwalking. (There is a dramatic case presented later)
10. Waking up with night sweats.
11. Also feeling cold or shivering in bed.

12. Waking up tired most mornings.

13. General fatigue and apathy.

14. Nausea in the morning, even vomiting.

15. General feelings of despondency, stress and depression.

16. Frequent crying upon waking up in the morning.

17. Rapid heartbeat while lying still in bed. Body cramps.

18. Lying down and feeling dizzy.

Naturally, one of these symptoms is sufficient to indicate a problem. However, there may be a multiplicity of symptoms appearing at the same time. If you are a health professional, a therapist, counselor or even a spiritual advisor who has heard from a client or patient any of the points mentioned above, remember to pose the following questions.

When did you move into the house or apartment?
When did you first start sleeping in the exact place where you now sleep?
When did your current condition first manifest itself?
Did the condition persist when you went away for a holiday, a business trip or spent a few days in hospital?
Did the condition return when you returned to your normal bed?

WATCH FOR ABNORMAL COMMENTS

If you are a homeowner, proud of your castle, there are some actions of which you might be aware:

Guests invited to dinner appear reluctant to sit at the table, and when they do they sit and eat in relative quiet with little conversation. It is almost as if an invisible damper has descended on them. When eating is finished they make comments such as "I need to stretch my legs," or "I'm feeling cold," or "Mabel. I get the feeling you don't use the dining room too much." Observe where guests congregate and feel comfortable.

Words to note. When your partner or a child or a relative comes up with the comment: "There's something odd about this house" or "I don't know what it is exactly, there's something here that should not be," take notice as if your life depends upon it, because being unaware of toxic Earth energy is maiming and killing more people than you can imagine and yes, pets.

PETS AND ANIMALS

Like humans our pets and animals are very much exposed to both beneficial and negative energies. Now there are some strange peculiarities here.

Dogs detest geopathic zones. If you put a dog's bed or kennel on a zone, the dog will avoid it even to the point of pretending he or she is hurt. If your dog sleeps on your bed — that's a good sign. The best strategy for helping dogs is to observe where they spend their time relaxing, sprawled out. That's the place to put a kennel, a basket of blankets. Your pet will appreciate it. Incidentally, if you are not into dowsing but are inclined to safe living, if there is a room upstairs over where your dog chooses to sleep, make that your bedroom. You will be glad you did.

If a cat spends hours on your bed curled up and sleeping it a grim warning sign. Cats love geopathic zones regardless of the fact it will eventually kill them. One lady whose home we cleared in Elmira NY reported that immediately after the clearing her cat suffered from an asthmatic attack. Some psychology experts suggest that asthma is a symptom of suppressed anger so it is possible the lady's cat was angry when it found out the geopathic stress zone was no longer running through the house. But the clearing may well have saved the creature's life.

Other creatures that love geopathic stress zones are ants, bees, wasps, rabbits, hornets, owls, snakes, mosquitoes, turtles, beavers, most insects, fungi, bacteria and mold. One creature that loves GSZ is the mole. If you spot a series of mole holes on your lawn or yard, chances are there's toxic energy underneath. For some strange reason negative energy to humans becomes a positive force for them.

Horses avoid the zones like the plague. If you keep or board a horse in a stable and he or she cannot move, they will create problems in a big way. A refusal to sleep is top, followed by kicking at everything particularly the stall walls and doors. They also create a lot of noise as if it's the end of the world. You will know if your horse has a zone problem.

But some older horses may not have the guts and kick to show their disapproval of the stable. They simply try to make the best of a bad existence. Such horses can suffer reduced immune systems and are then open to cancer and catastrophic disease. The answer is simply watch an older horse that stands listless and tired, yet perks up when outside with other animals. It's a signal something is not quite right in the stable.

It was a young woman's pride and joy, building her home and horse stables on a meadow she purchased near Carthage, NY. Connie was well aware that a nest of geospirals on the other side of the pond would radiate relaxing and healthful energy, plus we let her know a ley line, an old Indian track crossed her property. It would be a great place for a health spa! For her horses she cut no corners on their comforts. Warm stables included an indoor exercise ring, invaluable when the deep winter snows make outside exercise impossible.

"There's a problem," she called. "Two of the horses are kicking the place to pieces." On site, we found a geopathic zone running through the stable. Two breaker-rods were planted in the ground on both sides of the stable and that brought instant relief.

When it comes to GSZs horses are extremely sensitive to negative Earth radiation. They will let you know in no uncertain manner you have a problem. Cattle and other animals like goats, sheep, pigs and chickens will avoid toxic energy and make sorrowful and annoying sounds into the night that they do not wish to be there. In some European and Asian countries farmers use pigs to test whether some land is good for building new houses and barns. Pigs are good communicators to have around.

In the 1970s Dr Joseph Kopp, a noted Swiss dowser observed in a study the presence of subterranean water veins flowing under 130 barns. Every stall showed geopathic stress zones where horses and cows had developed illnesses such as rheumatism, miscarriages, uterine deterioration and in the case of dairy cows, a distinctly reduced milk yield . When the animals were moved out of the affected stalls, they eventually recovered. Healthy animals placed into the stalls quickly became sick.

Talking of horses, there's a strong equestrian movement in and around Abbotsford in the Fraser Valley of British Columbia. We heard that an equestrian stable had a history of losing horses to cancer in three of the stalls in one building. One local newspaper described them as "Sick stables".

When dowser Tom Passey and I responded to a call for help from a stable employee, we knew immediately there was a problem because the zone came out through the parking area and we both felt it. My feet became heavy and Tom suffered a brief pang of nausea so the geopathic stress zones were quickly marked.

A very official looking woman with an angry red face emerged from a house and when Tom offered to clear the zone free, she responded sharply: "We have had the best veterinary people and the best environmental experts and none of them have come up with a satisfactory conclusion.

I don't think water witches or wizards will do any good. We've sold the rest of our stock and putting the place up for sale."

"We can give you positive help," suggested Tom.

"No," she said firmly. "Besides it's against our beliefs."

Another case of disaster by belief. On the way home, Tom put it this way: "If your beliefs are so strong so that you don't believe in minefields, the minefields will come and kill you. If you don't believe in geopathic stress that too will send you on a journey to meet your maker."

TREES AND SIGNS OF STRESS

Our day to day environment contains various signs that geopathic stress zones are prevalent. The easiest to spot are trees. A comment we overheard in a park: "Oh, look at that tree. It's all bent out of shape. Isn't that cute? I must get a picture."

How was the young woman to know the tree was in agony and had been for most of its twenty or thirty years?

Trees growing on geopathic stress lines show their pains in different ways. Some trees appear malformed, their bark appears to rotate while some may also lean outward as if trying to escape from a nasty energy force. Others assume contorted shapes as if attempting to escape from excruciating pains that have them in their grasp. Others grow ugly warts, burrs or gnarls that stick out like sore thumbs. They are known as *tumor-type neoplasias.* (See PHOTOS #3 on page 108.)

Some trees particularly willows, oaks, redwoods, firs, elderberry, cherry, peach and mistletoe like and live well on geopathic stress zones. Beech, alder, birch, cedar dislike the zones and will display twisted forms indicating severe pain. Trees that show lack of growth, easy defoliation and demonstrate a lack of seeds or fruit could well be situated over a toxic energy vein. In addition trees on geopathic stress can be open to disease and infestations by ants. As mentioned earlier, ants and wasps (yellow-jackets) love geopathic stress zones. If you see a cluster of anthills, there's a GSZ lurking underneath. Some dowsers when clearing a house of toxic energies usually work to include a suffering tree.

If you are a vegetable or flower gardener you may find a certain area of the yard or garden where plants have difficulty growing in spite of ample water and fertilizer provided. Affected plants may appear to grow but fail to bear fruit. This also applies to apple and pear trees.

Another sign of toxic Earth energy that often appears on summer evenings is a tower of swirling gnats. Another indicator: animals that live underground often have tunnel openings on a geopathic stress zone. Why? Dogs and other predatory animals are reluctant to cross a geopathic stress zone. But so too are people.

INVISIBLE "DO NOT CROSS" SIGNS

A family trying to sell a home often have problems because a geopathic stress zone crosses the path or driveway. People hesitate to walk across the zone. They do not see it but "something inside" urges them not to cross. This phenomenon has been demonstrated time and time again.

A woman in Media, a college (Swarthmore) town near Philadelphia complained that her house, on the market for two years, was just not selling. Dowsing showed a double geopathic stress zone crossing her driveway. It was immediately cleared. This was Friday. On the following Sunday, an Open House attracted two dozen viewers, one of whom made a purchase.

By the way it is fair to point out that geopathic stress is not always to blame. It could be a negatively charged energy blocking the driveway.

This occurred on Canada's west coast where a man built a home on a lot next to his father's place. Eventually Dad died and the father's home was on the market for three long years.

Tom Passey checked and found a "negative energy cloud" hanging over the front gate. "While one part of the man wanted to sell the property, another part refused to let go," said Tom. "Unknowingly he created a negative energy that sat at the front gate effectively blocking visitors."

Tom used the Decree Technique to neutralize the unwanted energy. That technique, as we shall see, has formed a major activity in my life.

4

DRAGON BREATH AND SCIENCE

So who or what is this silent killer as seen in the eyes of Science? While Geopathic Stress is a relatively new name, created in the early 20th century, the phenomenon was known in the old days as Devil Fire, Dirty Dirt, Ugly Earth, and Dragon Breath. The energy and its problems were well known in the ancient Orient. Four thousand years ago when Kuang Yu was emperor of China he came to realize that dangerous Earth energies were emanating in different places, maiming and killing people and destroying families. The phenomenon was so prevalent he proclaimed an edict which is still in effect in China today: "No dwelling shall be built until the Earth diviners have confirmed the intended building site to be free of Earth demons."

There are various pictographs and carvings from ancient Egypt of men carrying rods complete with tasseled ribbons — divining rods — that quivered when the holder was over the target such as water veins and negative energy.

In the Holy Bible Moses used his rod at various times to find water and also to divide the Red Sea or the "Reed Sea" as some academics call it. These were no miracles simply a technique for moving energy and water.

Ancient Romans were very conscious of toxic earth energies. They would test areas for new buildings by having sheep graze on the planned site for a year. Afterwards the sheep were dissected to see if their inner organs were healthy or not. Roman architect and military engineer Marcus Vitruvius Pollio was well aware of geopathic stress, as was Hippocrates, long considered the father of western medicine, and Avicenna who was one of the most significant physicians, astronomers, thinkers and writers of the Islamic Golden Age. They were all concerned about the importance of location of buildings in relation to health.

Bavarians would install anthills in prospective bedrooms to see if the ants liked the place or ran away. If you have a number of ant hills close to your home, check the area for geopathic stress.

One technique from the ancient world of the Far East can be found in use today in parts of Europe. A diviner prepares two saucers with water both containing dissolved salt to saturation. One is placed in a suspected "bad earth" energy zone and the other in a good or neutral zone. After a few days the water evaporates and the salt examined. It will be found that the salt in the "bad earth" energy zone will have formed thick clumps of crystals devoid of harmony. The salt from the neutral zone will be evenly distributed and harmoniously structured.

HOW GEOPATHY TOOK SHAPE

The word "geopathy" was first coined by a Russian working in France. Georges Lakhovsky, who invented and patented the Multiple Wave Oscillator which is still in use today, first suggested in the 1930s that geopathic stress causes the human body to vibrate at much higher frequencies than normal and this can deleteriously affect the human immune system.

This, he said, makes people and animals sleeping or working in geopathically stressed locations more susceptible to virus, bacteria, parasites and environmental pollution. Lakhovsky is said to have cured himself of cancer.

An important point here: In the early days of modern scientists exploring dowsing and negative Earth energy it was easily ascribed that geopathic stress zones were the cause of cancer and various other catastrophic diseases. As science came to show, toxic Earth energy only targets and reduces the effectiveness of the immune system. Geopathic stress does not in itself create cancer, it weakens the immune system to the point that diseases and sickness prevail.

However it is difficult to explain to an unfortunate loved one dying of cancer that geopathic stress was not the cause of their plight. If a plane makes an emergency landing on a highway and hits a car which in turn strikes and damages your car and body do you blame the aircraft or the car that struck you? Lawyers and insurance folk might beat around the bush but the originating cause was the plane. The rest is pedantic.

SHE CALLED THEM "CANCER BEDS"

In the realm of dowsing and geopathic stress two names stand out as pioneers: Baron Gustav von Pohl and Käthe Bachler. Both connected geopathic stress zones and cancer, in fact Ms. Bachler coined the frightening term "cancer bed."

Vilsbiburg is a small town 42 miles north-east of Munich, Germany. In 1929 the townspeople requested von Pohl to dowse and survey the German community for geopathic stress because it had achieved the highest per capita cancer death rate in Bavaria. The dowser's survey produced a map of the toxic zones and then came the news that confirmed the people's suspicion.

Local hospital records showed that all 54 patients who had died of cancer since town medical records had been kept, had slept in beds above points marked on von Pohl's map. It was a 100% correlation.

When people glibly suggest this was not a scientific study, the opposite is true. Swiss Harmony, the European organization reports: During his investigation, von Pohl was not allowed to speak to any of his subjects and was accompanied continuously by a control group. Legal testimony confirms that the dowser did not know in advance whether or how many people died of cancer in Vilsbiburg. Yet, he succeeded in identifying the beds of all the 54 people who had died of cancer (32 male, 22 female).

Von Pohl published his findings in 1932 in a book titled "Erdstrahlen als Krankheitserreger — Forschungen auf Neuland" (Earth Currents–Causative Factors of Cancer and Other Diseases). It was republished in 1978 and is still commercially available.

In the following year 1930, he repeated the procedure in Grafenau, another Bavarian town which had the lowest incidence of cancer in the state and again found a 100 per cent correlation. If this was bad news, it was going to get worse.

When the Baron dowsed the death rate in the City of Stetten the results were horrifying. Dr. Harger, chairman of the city's medical scientific association declared that the "deadly earth currents" ran beneath the beds of all — 5,348 people — who had died from cancer over the past 21 years. During these studies, von Pohl developed a scale to rate Geopathic stress of 1 to 16, where a combined tally of 9 or above from streams crossing gives rise to cancer.

The von Pohl dowsing surveys inspired scientists and medical technologists to probe into the matter and the term Geobiology emerged and was adopted by some German dowsers. It represented the study of the relationship between life and the Earth's physical and chemical environment. This meant that Geobiologists came to specialize in surveying houses for both geopathic and electromagnetic stress using both dowsing and scientific instruments. Their hunch? There was more to geopathic stress zones that just toxic earth energy.

NOXIOUS VAPORS DISCOVERED

The late 1920s and early 1930s were years of investigation. French engineer Pierre Cody of Le Havre was well aware of local "cancer houses" because many citizens of the port city had died from cancer during those years. Being an engineer he knew of the gold leaf electroscope.

The electroscope was invented about the year 1600 by British physician William Gilbert to detect the presence and magnitude of an electric charge on a body. It was the first electrical measuring instrument. By the 1930s there existed the pith-ball electroscope and the gold-leaf electroscope, which are two classical types of electroscope still used in physics education today to demonstrate the principles of electrostatics. Electroscopes were used by the Austrian scientist Victor Hess in the discovery of cosmic rays.

So armed with the gold leaf electroscope Cody checked large numbers of cancer houses in Le Havre and found that the air in these deadly homes was ionized to an unusual degree. From various other tests Cody concluded that the ionized radiation consisted of positively charged Alpha Particles. Now, the only known source of alpha particle emission in dwellings is from Radon which is a naturally occurring radioactive gas. It is invisible and comes from the natural radioactive decay of uranium. It is usually found in igneous rock and soil, but in some cases, well water and subterranean water veins may also be a source of radon. Cody's early research appears to support Baron von Pohl's findings that noxious vapors and energies from underground water-bearing fissures were responsible for many of the cases of cancer.

In Britain a recent report from the National Radiological Protection Board (NRPB) estimates that out of 50,000 lung cancer deaths a year in the United Kingdom, radon gas is responsible for about 2,500 cases.

ENTER KÄTHE BACHLER

In dowsing research the name Käthe Bachler is world famous. An Austrian school teacher for thirty-two years, Ms. Bachler in the 1970s investigated Earth Radiation, flowing subterranean water veins, global magnetic fields and geological fault lines. Her work covered well over 18,000 sleeping places which produced astonishing results. The author of seven books, her most famous book in English is simply entitled "Earth Radiation".

In addition Ms. Bachler surveyed over 3,000 school children and found that children do not do well in geopathic stress zones, often being hyperactive and prone to allergies, asthma, attention deficit disorder and eczema. Some 95% of children who either slept or had their school desks on or near strong zones possessed learning difficulties, hyperactive tendencies or displayed continuous bad behavior. When the children were moved into stress free environments they nearly all displayed a marked improvement often going from bottom to top of their class in one term.

Ms. Bachler's studies showed that a very high proportion of children who were frequently absent, either sick or playing truant were in classrooms with geopathic stress zones and even among teachers there was a high rate of absenteeism. The survey also found that the majority of parents, relatives or guardians who abuse children are suffering from the effects of geopathic stress.

THE ROLLING CLASSROOM PROCEDURE

It is through Käthe Bachler that the "rolling classroom" student protection procedure came into being. In essence where there are geopathic stress zones in a classroom, students rotate their positions so they do not spend prolonged periods over toxic energy.

The Education Department of the Austrian school district of Salzburg even gave Ms. Bachler a research grant for her work and took her advice to introduce 'the rolling classroom' into their recommended procedure. This is an effective way to spread the radiation across various pupils substantially reducing its effect on the scholars in the process.

Today in many parts of Europe schools are no longer built until the Earth energy has been checked by dowsers and schools still in existence that were built over geopathic stress zones are carefully monitored. It was from Ms. Bachler's studies that such conditions as Attention Deficit Disorder (ADD) and Sudden Infant Death (SID) Syndrome can often be attributed to geopathic stress zones.

5

AMPLIFYING THE TOXIC ZONES

There are two phenomena of which the dowser and energy hunters should be aware: the Curry Net and the Hartman Grid. Some sources say both were named after their discoverers but it is not so. The Curry Net was named in 1952 after Dr. Manfred Curry a German doctor and famous yachtsman, but he was not the discoverer. That was the work of Siegfried Wittmann in 1950.

Their existence covers the Earth and normally they are not much trouble. The problem emerges when geopathic stress zones cross the nodal points of the net or grid. Grid negativity points are intensified.

The Curry Net's zones of disturbance equate to the intermediate compass points — that is they run from North-East to South-West and from South-East to North-West and vice versa. As a rule they run triangularly, but sometimes shift diagonally.

The grid varies according to where you stand on the planet. If you are on or about the 49th parallel — the Canadian-U.S. border — the grid lines occur every 2.75 to 3 meters. Closer to the equator, the distance between lines ranges from 4.5 to 5 meters. The further north one travels the lines are closer together. If that is confusing, here is another point: The width of the lines vary according to the weather.

Dr. Curry distinguished that the grid has two types of intersections: One has a charging effect (+), the other a discharging effect (-). He found that positive intersections enhanced cell enlargement and cell proliferation in humans, even to the point of cancerous growth. At the negative intersection, the energy enhanced inflammations.

On their own, the lines or bands have little negative effect. The problems occur only at the Curry crossing points. The effect is intensified where the net meets with hazardous subterranean water currents, to the point that people sleeping on such places will find themselves suffering from insomnia, morning fatigue, restlessness, night-tremors and night-sweating. Prolonged living on such points can produce catastrophic diseases, particularly cancer and ultimately death.

For the practicing dowser bent on clearing a house it is sufficient to tune into "all the toxic or hazardous energies" under one command. The logic is to capture and eliminate the entire negative field. In other words it is relatively worthless to address Curry crossings and geopathic stress zones separately, unless a scientific survey is being conducted. A general clearing to make a home or office safe and livable must be all embracing such as "all negative and harmful energies be transmuted and converted to that which is good and beautiful."

THE ERNST HARTMAN GRID

The Hartmann Grid was discovered by the German physician Ernst Hartmann in 1954 and described in detail in his book "Krankheit als Standortproblem" (Illness as a Location Problem). The Grid is associated with the Earth's magnetic field and is therefore more Cosmic than the Curry Net. It comprises a mass of standing waves about 20 centimeters or eight inches wide. The lines run in a north-south and east-west direction and are set between two and 2.5 meters apart.

The interesting point about the Hartman Grid is that the lines tend to move with (1) the time of day, (2) the weather, and (3) when they are found in the vicinity of rocks and water. They can also be deflected by crystalline rocks planted at ground level or just below the surface, and also by metal stakes driven into the ground.

A strange phenomenon occurs with the Hartmann Grid. It occurs when surplus electrical energy, offshoots from electrical equipment at industries, farms and indeed large apartment complexes where electrical systems are grounded, can actually gather and flow along Hartmann waves.

In this way they can impact the immune systems of animals such as horses, cattle, goats, pigs and also humans living and sleeping directly above the grid lines.

As mentioned earlier, the Curry Grid lines on their own have little negative effect. The problem occurs only at the Curry crossing points which alternate negative and positive. In short, this is a double whammy of negativity on the Earth and the human body's Schumann Resonance of 7.83 Hz. As Dr. Hartman discovered the scale gets blown anywhere up to a dangerous 250 Hz.

An outline of Dr. Hartmann's life is worth noting because his theories would be tested by the University of Vienna, as we shall see.

Ernst Hartmann was born in November 1915 at Waldkatzenbach in Germany and became a medical doctor, an author and dowser. After leaving school, Hartmann studied medicine in Mannheim and Jena. During World War II he worked as a staff physician and was in American captivity. After his return from captivity, he opened a medical practice in Eberbach — also known as Baden on the river Neckar, where he worked for more than 40 years as a practitioner.

Besides his work as a doctor, in 1948, Ernst Hartmann still studied together with his brother Robert with geobiology and dowsing. Furthermore, he occupied himself with homeopathy and later biology. He founded the registered organization known as the Research Group for Geobiology.

But Dr. Hartmann, who died in Mannheim on 23 October 1992, is best known for his theory and work on the Hartmann Line or Grid. A dowser scanning for geopathic stress zones is always advised to ask if the zones are intersected by a negative Hartmann Grid point which will intensify the negative energy. Three years before he passed on, the University of Vienna using both dowsers and scientists tested Hartmann's theory.

UNDER THE MICROSCOPE

As a dowser when I hear prominent writers on influential newspapers declare in articles that "dowsing has not been scientifically proved" I used to chuckle, now I am horrified over their abysmal ignorance of the facts: dowsing and science have worked together over many years on many "scientific studies". Here's how.

In 1989 Dr. Ernst Hartmann's theory was tested by a group of researchers in Austria who completed a two-year study on the short term consequences of human association with pathogenic lines. Some 985 people were tested and various data was collected from 6,943 individual tests. Dr. Otto Bergsmann, internal medicine professor at the University of Vienna headed the working party.

The research was conducted by a team of distinguished professors, doctors, engineers, scientists and dowsers. To test the hypothesis three dowsers known for their expertise in locating Earth energies were brought in.

They were asked to independently dowse eight different locations, submit reports and diagrams of the strongest geopathic stress points labeled "Disturbed Zones" together with a "Neutral Zone" at the same location. This enabled researchers to carry out double blind experiments with volunteers at each selected location. The dowsers found that the greatest pathogenic influences came from the movement of underground streams, Hartmann/Curry global grid lines and geological fault lines.

In order to rule out possible influences of human made electromagnetic or microwave disturbances at each location, an independent report from an electromechanical engineer was requested for each chosen site.

The project tested 24 different biological parameters involving 985 trial volunteers in 6,943 investigations using 462,421 individual measurements. Volunteers with any degree of sickness were released.

The test results were lined up by Biometric Significance and valued by Serotonin alteration. In essence, research suggests that serotonin plays an important role in regulating mood, appetite, sleep and dreaming. It can achieve both a sedating or stimulating effect which is somehow related to the flow of thoughts through the mind.

How technical can they get? In the lead position they measured the decline speed of Blood Corpuscle and Immunoglobulin deficiencies. Serotonin decreased by a factor of 6 on the "Disturbed Zone" while increasing its metabolism to advance Tryptophan in compensation. "This reaction was highly significant" stated the report.

(Immunoglobulin is any of a class of proteins present in the serum and cells of the immune system that function as antibodies.) The three Immunoglobulins that were examined: IgA, IgG and IgM showed clear reactions on the geopathic stress zones. Immunoglobulin IgA showed the highest significant drop. When tested on the "Neutral Zone" the values appeared normal. In Blood Sedimentation Speed: Blood Corpuscle decline speed slowed down while on the "Disturbed Zone."

The Vienna Report stated the research team concluded there was no evidence to relate "Disturbed Zones" to a specific illness. In other words, the team concluded what dowsers have theorized all along: *Geopathic Stress Zones reduce the effectiveness of the human and animal immune systems.*

The research group has now linked with two universities in Austria studying the effects of disturbed zones on the immune system. Indications so far support the findings of Dr. Ernst Hartmann who claimed that "the protective role of the immune system is determined when immersed in emissions of detrimental earth radiation".

In 1995, a new seven year study with over 8,200 patients was conducted by the Institute of Geopathology and Naturopathy in Kassel, Germany. It evaluated the effects of Geopathic Stress on people's health.

One key finding: *Any medical treatment, be it traditional or alternative, appeared to be drastically prolonged or even blocked as a result of Geopathic Stress Zones. As soon as these structures were avoided or shielded against, the medical treatment promptly resumed and showed positive results.*

This is often the case in many U.S. states. A person, innocently suffering from a catastrophic disease because they are sleeping on a geopathic stress zone, is taken to hospital for treatment. Medical staff find there is often a sudden improvement in the person's health. It happens: The patient is sent home and that is like a death sentence. Within a few days or sometimes hours the suffering begins anew.

Does anyone ever stop to think the problem might be in the Earth under the bed?

As the University of Vienna an intensive study showed that geopathic stress inhibits neurotransmitters, especially serotonin, which in this state can lead to mood dysfunction, depression and apathy. Rarely do people realize that negative feelings are manifestations of geopathic stress, and if you avoid these geopathic zones, the symptoms and feelings can be permanently eliminated. Serotonin comes up later in chapter six of this notebook regarding SIDS — Sudden Infant Deaths Syndrome.

BREAKDOWN OF THE IMMUNE SYSTEM

Which illness may you risk by prolonged exposure to strong zones of disturbance? Von Pohl, Käthe Bachler, Ole Hovmand, Rolf Gordon and other researchers and doctors listed illnesses that most often occur. Remember, these conditions are not caused by harmful earth rays, but develop because of the breakdown of the body's natural functioning and lowering of the immune system.

Cancer, aids, arthritis, rheumatism, asthma, migraine, insomnia, many stomach, kidney, bladder, liver and gallbladder disorders, tuberculosis, multiple sclerosis, heart conditions, diabetes, sinus, uterus and adrenals conditions, osteoarthritis, thrombosis, eyes, ears and teeth disorders, inflammations, varicose veins, leukemia, emotional and mental disorders.

There is strong evidence that links earth rays with suicide, divorce, depression, stress, high blood pressure and alcoholism.

One illness we came across directly in researching and writing this book is alopecia areata a condition where the body attacks its own hair follicles. A boy's parents were really concerned, so in late 2017 we cleared the geopathic stress from the house in Italy. Four months later we heard from his mother: "Here everything is fine. Pietro's hair issue is really slowly but steadily improving. I hope it will go on improving and I'm confident it will."

Often if children are present in geopathicallly stressed homes there can be clear indications of depression. Someone, normally a teenager becomes chronically depressed and on medication is a good example. What is more, they do not have to be directly on the path of the negative rays, their young bodies sense the proximity of the zones, absorb the presence and respond accordingly.

The National Institute of Mental Health says depression is the most common mental health disorder in the United States among teens and adults. 2.8 million youths aged 12-17 had at least one major depressive episode in 2014. Between 10 to 15 percent of teenagers have some symptoms of teen depression at any one time.

In our dowsing of geopathic stress zones we often find teens suffering depression and when a parent is questioned the reply is almost always the same: "He always feels better in someone else's house or when he's on an out-of-town event or away on vacation." One mother added: "That always makes us feel guilty that we are not providing the best home environment."

Some parents, particularly women look to unconventional modalities to improve the home. Psychics, yogis, shamans, healers are brought in, often at a substantial cost and the home is scoured for any negative energies such as EMF, negative entities, ley lines, remains of an Indian burial site, and of course feng shui which is a Chinese system of energy laws (qi) used when positioning and designing buildings. Rarely, if ever, does anyone ever consider looking or feeling under the beds. It is as if what goes on under the bed is hallowed ground and not to be violated.

THE CRYSTALS DILEMNA

Many people when afflicted by negative Earth radiation turn to crystals in hopes of clearing the unwanted affects of geopathic stress or associated negativity. A moderate number of well studied and selected crystals can help the owner maintain a good and beneficial energy in the home.

Naturally some critics scoff at the idea of using crystals for healing, completely forgetting that crystals such as quartz, silicon, galena, pyrite and others are widely used in sonar, ultrasound, radios, transistors, digital watches, amplifiers in electric guitars, microphones, gas-powered appliances such as ovens, heaters and even lighters. Computers, tablets, cell phones and televisions — all contain crystals either in solid or liquid form.

The problem is some people, frantic for help in combating feelings of negative energy in the home go overboard and amass large numbers of crystals. A woman in one house we visited in rural Pennsylvania possessed a large 36 inch bowl loaded with every crystal imaginable. At the same time she vigorously expressed concerns about the EMF radiation from the electronic measuring device outside her house and claimed it was causing her "mental and physical exhaustion."

We found two geopathic stress zones running through the home and while that was bad news, the bowl of crystals actually amplified the toxic impact of the geopathic zones. It would have been interesting to have had a medical practitioner measure her serotonin levels. To add to this toxic energy hodge-podge, outside in the front yard were five geospirals radiating healthful Yin energy like a mini-vortex.

Dowsing the influence of the crystal collection showed its area of influence was a quarter of a mile in any direction and amplified the two geopathic stress zones so they covered the entire house. We cleared the place of toxic earth energies and advised her to place the bowl of crystals in a distant shed or storeroom, or break up the collection, keeping only those required to maintain optimal health.

Moderation in all things. When selecting crystals ask your pendulum: "Is this crystal good for my health now?" Always listen to your Higher Consciousness and not the Ego Mind.

UNDERSTANDING AN ENERGY DILEMMA

Many illustrators of geopathic stress zones often draw them in straight lines and this is far from being accurate. The zones are as different as people. They do change as rivers, creeks and ditches squiggle or wander across the landscape and yes, they do change their courses over time.

These points came from a question raised by Carol of Lawrenceville N.J. who asked if geopathic stress zones change over time. The answer of course is "yes." The ones that can and do change are often seasonal because they are near the surface, perhaps two or three feet to 20 feet below. Activated by late winter and spring run-offs and summer storms they may only exist for a few weeks to several months and may or may not reappear next year.

Seasonal zones are as temperamental and as unpredictable as the weather in winter and often as difficult to explain to a sufferer of fibromyalgia. In dowsing the operator should always enquire: Is this subterranean water vein permanent or seasonal?

So-called permanent geopathic stress zones depend solely on the subterranean water vein and its environment. They usually exist from just a few feet underground to over 1,200 feet down and rarely if ever change. A minor earth tremor, drilling for oil or a water well, may prompt a change as will gradual changes in clay, rocks and fissures.

While temporary geopathic zones are narrow water veins — eight to 12 inches wide, the permanent ones, deep down can be anywhere from 12 inches to 30 inches wide and more. They can exist in caves and gullies deep underground.

We cleared one in Mount Holly, New Jersey that was half a mile long, 900 feet down and in places four to five feet wide — almost as if there were little ponds. Such ponds accumulate stagnant water which leach chemicals from rocks and have varying effects on the toxic energy produced.

Now, here is a dilemma Carol raised. When there is a subterranean water vein sending noxious rays up through an apartment building and there are a couple of geospirals immediately outside, radiating beneficial Yin energy across the building, why is not the geopathic stress neutralized?

My theory is that both energies work separately on the human or animal form. In fact the inhabitants of the apartments may be lulled into a pleasant form of relaxation little knowing there is a geopathic stress zone undermining their immune system, which may or may not collapse at some future date. To be lulled into a relaxed state like that is similar to a thug armed with a pistol presenting you with a bouquet of flowers just before taking your wallet or purse.

It is important therefore, that dowsers on assignment scanning for geopathic stress zones also be alert to the existence and close proximity of geospirals, particularly the larger and stronger ringed ones — 21 to 49 — that may hide from the inhabitants the dangers inherent in a GSZ. In other words, the Silent Killer Below is working under the shade of beautiful feminine geospiral energy.

A similar dilemma can also apply if a home flanks a ley line. The average ley produces a zone of beautiful and beneficial Yin energy that can cover a swathe of 100 yards. One lady who felt there was "something wrong" with her home, not only had a double geopathic stress zone in the house, but was within the Area of Influence of a triple-haired ley line in the street outside. If someone mistakenly claims that a nearby ley is negative or "evil" the dowser would do well to check for a geopathic stress zone lurking under the dwelling.

I recently came across an esteemed U.K. writer who told her readers that leys were created by people. If this were so, every city, town and village would possess leys. They do not.

History has shown that our ancient ancestors built their sacred temples, pyramids, cathedrals, churches and their communities where two or more leys crossed. If the reader would like to learn more on leys obtain a copy of my opus "Chasing the Cosmic Principle: Dowsing from Pyramids to Back Yard America."

(There is a "beneficial energy" section at the end of this notebook on geospirals and leys.)

6

AWARENESS ON THE HOME FRONT

Recall the major study of Dr. Otto Bergsmann, internal medicine professor at the University of Vienna? In 1989 he conducted scientific studies that showed geopathic stress zones affect serotonin levels in the human body.

In July 2017 the Eunice Kennedy Shriver National Institute of Child Health and Human Development issued a report which said blood samples from infants who died of Sudden Infant Death Syndrome (SIDS or Crib Death) had high levels of Serotonin.

The study, led by Robin L. Haynes Ph.D., of Boston's Children's Hospital and Harvard Medical School was funded by the National Institute. "In the current study, the researchers reported that 31 per cent of SIDS infants — 19 of 61 — had elevated blood levels of serotonin," said the report. "In previous studies, researchers reported multiple serotonin-related brain abnormalities in SIDS cases, including a decrease in serotonin in regions involved in breathing, heart rate patterns, blood pressure, temperature regulation and arousal during sleep."

Taken together, the researchers wrote: "The findings suggest that an abnormality in serotonin metabolism could indicate an underlying vulnerability that increases SIDS risk and that testing blood samples for serotonin could distinguish certain SIDS cases from other infant deaths." Then they added: "more research is needed."

The Haynes Report appeared in the Proceedings of the National Academy of Sciences and it appears no one had heard of the University of Vienna Report findings in Europe a quarter of a century before and if they did, it was ignored.

INFANTS WILL SAY 'SOMETHING IS WRONG'

Everyone is endowed with instinctive, intuitive or psychic gifts, but few people choose to use them, relying instead on intellectual arguments that fail to sense beneficial or harmful energies around. It is like many humans playing a game of Russian Roulette with death.

This is why most new home-owners have no idea that a geopathic stress zone is flowing through their property. First signs may be a young child upon being put to bed simply cries and cries, driving and forcing the parents to go beyond the parameters of love and patience.

One young mother said: "My husband could not sleep, I held the boy until he was asleep, then placed him back in his crib. Five minutes later he was crying like before. We both lost sleep and it affected our work and our marriage. It was a doctor who told us to get a dowser to check the crib for dirty energy."

Juniors may plead to sleep with parents or older siblings, or they may be found coiled up at the far end of the crib or they may be found sleeping on the floor at the far side of the bedroom — anything to get away from something bothering them in bed.

Some parents who have lost babies to this shattering phenomenon have later discovered the crib was on a geopathic stress zone.

Occasionally when a parent stubbornly believes nothing is wrong, and suggests the child is "stubborn" or "just playing with us," would be well advised to spend a while in the child's bed.

Here's an exercise for a doubting parent: Lie down on the child's bed, make yourself comfortable, close your eyes and take in three slow deep breaths. Really fill up the lungs and take your time. You will find this exercise alone relaxes you. Then say: "I am going to slowly count backwards from ten down to one, and when I reach number one I will feel as if I have slept in this bed for eight hours."

Perform the exercise slowly and see how your body and mind feel afterwards. When you are ready, take in a slow deep breath and as you breathe out, say the words "Wide awake!" and be wide awake. Be honest and note how you feel. You may be quite surprised.

SIMPLE SOLUTION FOR IMMEDIATE RELIEF

If you come to realize that "something is wrong" with a bed and people are suffering symptoms explained earlier, one simple solution is to move the bed.

A pendulum will readily indicate the presence of a geopathic stress zone. It will also tell you of a safe place to which you can move the bed.

A digital age indicator of geopathic stress can be found in a Smartphone. Go to Google apps and download a compass. Check that it works fine, then walk through the affected bedroom. When the Smartphone is over a geopathic stress zone the needle will swing violently. In this way you can become an electronic dowser. Anyway, once the zone is located you can move the bed to safety.

Here's a peculiar note: Some people who vacate a home or an apartment because "there's something there," are more than likely to find another place to live with a full blown geopathic stress zone in attendance. Strange? Absolutely, but true.

From time to time, a person looking for a new dwelling will email and ask us to check various addresses. Out of three options, two contain geopathic stress which we offer to move. The third is clean and appears very attractive. So they pick one I have to clear. But before the request for clearing comes over, they have to live in it to "test" the place. If you think dowsers are weird, try ordinary people!

Käthe Bachler mentions a similar pattern in her book that if you attempt to move a chronically sick person off a geopathic stress zone, the person will often complain and want the bed moved back to the original location. The solution here is to gradually move the bed a couple of inches at a time until it is in a safe place. Apparently — honest deceit works.

PLASTIC TO THE RESCUE

For the inhabitant of a small roomed apartment where moving the bed is impossible, there is a temporary remedy. Plastic sheet is a well known psychic energy blocker. Find several full size garbage bags. Lift up the mattress and place one layer of bags so it completely covers the box spring. Replace the mattress and make the bed. This will bring immediate relief but it will last only about three months. What to do? Get some fresh garbage bags and replace the old ones.

Another point to watch for: If you have an old bed with an iron frame, wire netting, and a mattress with wire springs, you cannot move the bed, and are plagued by a geopathic stress, do not bother with plastic. The bed amplifies the toxic effects. Get a new bed, then get plastic or find a new place to live, or call a dowser to clear the place. This information comes from 1987 scientific studies in Austria.

PROTECTION OUTSIDE OF DOWSING

For those who do not like to dowse or prefer a technological defense system there are many offerings on the market. Do they work? Some people affirm while others say no. Here's what we are told and all are designed to clear a home or an office from harmful vibrations. These tools can be found under such names as Space Harmonizers, Pyramids, Energy Plates, Geo Resonators. Apparently there are some devices that employ lasers to protect the home from toxic energy.

There is a wide variety of personal energy tools to help strengthen your energy and protect from geopathic stress as well as EMF radiation. These tools are made by using various types of technologies, materials and designs. You can find them under various names, from Personal Protection Pendants to Bio-Shield or Bio-Resonance Pendants, Tesla Pendants, and others.

Most of the geopathic stress personal protection tools come as pendants made with crystals, silver or gold. Some look very attractive and can be worn as jewelry, and some are worn unnoticed. The price range is anywhere from $45 for a simple pendant to over $300 USD for a pendant made from gold; you can find a variety of options and information on-line.

Because this is a relatively new field, be sure to research it well and compare not only the prices but also the effectiveness of each tool that might help you. As with everything new, do not hesitate to ask as many questions as needed in order to make the right choice. Use your pendulum and Higher Consciousness for decisive issues.

Some critics may argue that personal pendants and crystals are not aligned to work against geopathic stress, EMF or radon radiation. A mystical answer would be anything will work providing there is intent by the wearer or indeed the creator or manufacturer. It is best for the wearer to create the intent — in other words see, feel and think of the device providing perfect protection.

Alternatively ask the Creator the Source of Your Being, the Cosmic Forces, Infinite Intelligence or whoever you believe holds the powers of the Universe to provide protection through whatever device you choose to wear.

The Mind is a powerful communicator. Later in this book you will read how to clear a home of toxic energy simply by using your mind — and a decree!

7

THE WORKPLACE AND "SICK" BUILDINGS

Geopathic stress zones are not limited to homes. They crop up anywhere in such places as offices, factories, hotels, stores, shopping centers and more. If you notice a store or restaurant changes ownership every few months you can be assured a geopathic stress zone lurks somewhere. This also applies to apartments and rental homes. People will actually pull down a building and rebuild it hoping to remove an "stigma" that might have been inherent in the old place. Little knowing the problem still lurks in the soil.

The Dulwich Health Society (UK) checked over 25,000 people with ill health and found the following:

> 95% of cancer patients live and/or work in a Geopathic Stress environment.
>
> 95% of children who are hyperactive live in a Geopathic Stress environment.
>
> 80% of women who miscarry live or work in a Geopathic Stress environment.

80% of people who get divorced live in a Geopathic Stress environment.

Various doctors in Europe who between them have investigated over 10,000 cancer patients found 92% were living in a Geopathic Stress environment.

If you have ever come across the initials M.E., you will know they stand for Myalgic Encephalomyelitis, commonly known as chronic fatigue syndrome (CFS). It affects 250,000 Britons and is slightly more common in women than men. Roger A. Rose. FIMCS, MAA, MS, a bio med practitioner in Dunstable, England over a period of three years treated over 50 M.E. sufferers and found all of his M.E. patients were geopathically stressed.

M.E. is even more pronounced in the United States. The Center for Disease Control and Prevention reports that at least one million Americans suffer from ME/CFS and the costs to society including individuals, their families, caregivers, employers and society are estimated to be between $18 to $51 billion annually. The CDC report says although more common in women, ME/CFS affects people of all ages, including children, and people of all races and ethnicities. Internationally, scientists have not discovered the cause of ME/CFS but existing research shows most if not all sufferers are geopathically stressed.

A PRACTITIONER'S NOTE FROM IRELAND

While the Center for Disease Control in the United States does not officially recognize geopathic stress, the subject has come up in one of its forums held by the National Institute for Occupational Safety and Health (NIOSH). Geopathic stress exists on one page in a printed forum that embraces 2,714 pages. Incidentally, NIOSH is a U.S. federal agency that conducts research and makes recommendations to prevent worker injury and illness.

The lonely contributor, who signs himself Con Colbert , writes: *"My interest is in Health and Safety in the general environment with two aspects of the environment in mind.*

I carry out surveys in homes and workplaces for Radiation - Technical (Man-made) Electromagnetic influences and natural (but distorted) radiation from the earth which cause areas of disturbed energies commonly known as "geopathic zones".

Both of these influences contribute to the overall radiation load in the working and living environment with very serious consequences for human health and well-being.

One of the worst cases I encountered was a young woman who, after giving birth to her eldest child (son), gave birth to two babies with severe deformities and parts of the body missing. Both died within 8 weeks of birth. The environmental source of her problem was her workplace.

Having located the source, my advice was to move her workplace to another part of the office. She did so and subsequently gave birth to a healthy daughter. When her first child was born she had worked in a different office in another part of the building. Among the illnesses that I have come across are the following; cancer, leukaemia, CFS(ME), depression, general malaise /fatigue, digestive upsets, allergies, ibs (irritable bowel syndrome), asthma, immune suppression. Two of the childhood leukaemia cases I came across are living normal healthy lives after 3 & 8 years respectively. Where there is doubt or uncertainty about the aetiology of an illness, the living and working environments must be examined for the aforementioned influences. The solution can, in most cases be as simple as moving a work-station or a bed. Yours, Con Colbert, Dublin, Ireland." (Editor: A good letter but the writer could be using an historical pseudonym)

"SICK BUILDING" SYNDROME

In 1983, the World Health Organization (WHO) used the term "Sick Building Syndrome" for the first time to describe situations in which building occupants experience acute health and discomfort effects that appear to be linked to the time spent in a building, but no specific illness or cause can be identified. Many, including the WHO, believe that SBS is the main cause of absence from work and low efficiency of staffs and employees.

People who sit at office desks for many hours and such places are located on narrow zones of disturbance, will usually feel uncomfortable, and gradually the total productivity and speed of their work will diminish, as well as work quality.

In one large hair dressing salon in Watertown N.Y., a geopathic stress zone ran through the receptionist's desk and chair. The salon owner commented: "That's probably why we have had four receptionists in 12 months."

How did we discover this problem? During our time in upstate New York, Betty Lou and I were regular customers and we could not help feeling the toxic energy running through the waiting room and the receptionist's office. We checked, and sure enough there was a geopathic stress zone. With their permission we promptly cleared it.

While business owners seem reluctant to talk to dowsers or energy workers, employees become frustrated with frequent aches suffered at work places. Such was the case of Elli who said her health industry company has "suffered many set backs since moving to this location." She wrote that employees "took a 10 per cent wage cut due to the problems. Personally I have felt extra tired and had stomach and headaches."

On behalf of the staff, Elli gave us permission to clear and it happened. Two days later Elli wrote: "Thank you for clearing my workspace. Thank you from the bottom of my heart."

But businesses are not easy to deal with. Visits to a bank on State Highway 38 near Mount Holly, New Jersey always caused Betty Lou to come home complaining that the staff members were edgy and not all that cooperative. A scan on Google Earth revealed a geopathic stress zone coming across the State Highway and splitting into a Y-shaped configuration in the bank. Betty Lou took a print of the scan to show the manager.

"We have had some problems here," acknowledged the manager who then promptly contacted the property owner. The woman replied that she would call us with permission to clear. She never did and we are still waiting.

As dowsers we respect everyone's privacy — home dwellers as well as business owners. Some business people are cooperative. When another bank manager told us he was moving to another bank off Route 38 where "they have had some problems," he asked if we would check out the place. We found a geopathic stress zone and cleared it for him. An employee, he took responsibility and gave us permission. It should have been the owner.

The bottom line is this, if you are a business owner and you are witnessing an unusual turnover in staff, or not so many customers are coming through your front door, have a dowser check for geopathic stress zones. If they live nearby most dowsers will clear it for nothing. Some dowsers, who work remotely will check, report and clear for a small fee. Remote clearing which is effective and permanent is described later.

Incidentally, people whose permanent places of work are located above a radiation-free area, often report feelings of well-being and tend to work faster, have greater capacities for work, and produce higher quality work.

MOLD AND GEOPATHIC STRESS

According to the Center for Disease Control and Prevention: "There is always some mold everywhere — in the air and on many surfaces. Molds have been on the Earth for millions of years. Mold grows where there is moisture."

Exposure to damp and moldy environments may cause a variety of health effects, or none at all. Some people are sensitive to molds. For these people, molds can cause nasal stuffiness, throat irritation, coughing or wheezing, eye irritation or, in some cases, skin irritation.

The CDC writes: People with mold allergies may have more severe reactions. Immune-compromised people and people with chronic lung illnesses, such as obstructive lung disease, may get serious infections in their lungs when they are exposed to mold. These people should stay away from areas that are likely to have mold, such as compost piles, cut grass, and wooded areas.

In 2004 the Institute of Medicine (IOM) found there was sufficient evidence to link indoor exposure to mold with upper respiratory tract symptoms of coughing and wheezing in otherwise healthy people with asthma symptoms and with hypersensitivity pneumonitis in individuals susceptible to that immune-mediated condition. The IOM also found limited or suggestive evidence linking indoor mold exposure and respiratory illness in otherwise healthy children.

What many dowsers have known for years is that when mold is evident in any house, well ventilated or not, there is a pronounced chance of a geopathic stress zone lurking somewhere. The problem is that when geopathic stress is born from Earth energy passing through a subterranean water vein it produces toxic rays that are aquated. In other words you may have a dry, well ventilated home but the geopathic stress gets linked to inherent moisture in floorboards, wooden walls. In fact, you may think everything in your home is dry.

Laura lives with her husband in a fine country home in Chadds Ford, Pennsylvania. A fifty-year old stone and brick home set in acres of rolling lawns, trees, fishponds, a gazebo and stone pathways.

"It's mold," she said. "It keeps coming back. The experts keep returning and eliminating it but then a few months later, back it comes. Can dowsing help?"

We walked the entire perimeter of the house and found one geopathic line running into the house and exiting on the far side by the garage. Inside, the dowsing rods showed the zone went through a large bedroom including the bed, a large antique wooden framed affair.

"That's where the mold is. Underneath!" she said defiantly. "It's just started to come back and I've tried every cleaner in the book. Can you do something?"

Outside on the lawns on both side of the house we planted breaker-rods on the geopathic stress zone. Instantly, it diverted the toxic rays in an arc over the house. Back inside, the bedroom was clear of geopathic stress.

A month later, Laura called: "Your trick worked. What was there disappeared and there's been nothing ever since. I'll call you if it ever comes back."

Laura never called so one must presume the "trick" worked.

MOLD IN THE SCHOOLS

In the late summer of 2017 the news media carried a string of stories concerning the plight of Holly Glen, an elementary school at Williamstown, New Jersey. As 500 children returned to school after the summer holidays, mold was found rampant in certain parts of the school. The building was immediately closed and environmental specialists called in.

In October the school and the mold were still making news. Curious, we dowsed the place on Google Earth and quickly discovered an H-shape configuration of geopathic stress zones crossing the north-east section of the building. The school was almost deserted when we arrived carrying a print of the geopathic stress. A school maintenance manager at the north end stopped to listen. Staring at the photo he said: "That's exactly where the mold is. I'll pass this on." (See PHOTOS #11 on page 112.)

"We can clear it as a public service," we told him.

We never did hear from anyone in authority. The school remained closed for months while the 500 students attended three other area schools. On December 13th 2017 School district officials announced they had decided to keep Holly Glen elementary school closed for the remainder of the school year because of the severe mold problems.

What happened? The environmental company originally mentioned to clean up the school no longer appeared. Holding some prints of the geopathic stress zones we visited their offices in Moorestown, N.J. A manager said bluntly: "We cannot say anything. We do not have that as a project."

When the subject of geopathic stress zones was mentioned he did respond "We'll have to look into that," but when I attempted to explain dowsing and clearance, he responded: "Look, I'm very busy," and promptly disappeared. One could nicely call it "rejection", but I felt it was like trying to sell a dead horse at a Church fund-raising party.

An Industrial Engineer later explained: "You have to appreciate that the college training centers set specific parameters for environmental technicians and engineers and very few are willing to explore outside those boundaries."

"Even though an abnormal or unusual technique may be successful?"

"Yes. Absolutely! They fear working outside of their boxes."

"Even though it may save lives — and money."

"Absolutely!"

The Superintendent of Monroe Township Public Schools, including Holly Glen was Charles M. Earling Jr. We emailed a detailed letter to him offering our services but he never replied. It was early in February 2018, the same day that a citizens group launched a petition calling for him and two supporting managers to resign over the school mold and closure issue.

A quiet request for clearing would have eliminated the geopathic stress zones immobilizing the school, and perhaps an ugly petition. It would have been so easy.

A long-time friend of Betty Lou who was living in South Jersey said she had suffered mold in her home and paid $11,000 for its removal. "Now it's back. Can you help?"

Dowsing on Google Earth showed a geopathic stress zone and it was quickly cleared and has not returned.

When it comes to mold and dowsing one is treading on the sacred beliefs of not only personal ideals but also commercial stigmas. Incidentally, in England and countries that formed the old British Empire the word mold is spelled mould.

8

DEALING WITH THE SILENT KILLER

In this electronic and digital age there are many devices and gadgets for finding and eliminating geopathic stress zones and while this is wonderful news for the people afflicted there is one major hang-up, most of them find and eliminate for a short duration.

Various cultures have displayed different methods of breaking or neutralizing geopathic stress zones. In Germany iron stakes were placed in the ground at the four corners of a house. The theory was and still is that iron stakes act like lightning rods, they attract geopathic energy and dissipate it.

Another ploy: an iron stake or a metallic hoop is placed on the direct path of a geopathic stress zone and it diverts the toxic energy round the building to rejoin the flow path. Apparently this technique produces an onion-shaped flow round the affected building.

In Eastern Europe people would plant garlic or mint in the areas of a negative energy zone. We have explored other techniques for diverting or neutralizing geopathic stress and these are featured later.

Once homes are cleared, residents often ask "Is it permanent? Will it come back?" We strive for permanence and in the strategies outlined ahead, this is our target: Permanent eradication or complete elimination.

BREAKER RODS AND MUDDY BOOTS DOWSING

This is the tried and true technique used by many dowsers for countless years. It demands travel, dowsing and physical work and the reward one gets is to meet and talk to people affected. It is the band of brothers and sisters I like to call the "Muddy Boots Dowsers."

For this traditional mode of dowsing you will need some equipment. A pair of L-rods (not too long or they get blown around in the wind), a pendulum, good walking shoes or boots, a small sledge-hammer, some landscape markers (little colored flags from hardware stores) and — a nifty and necessary object known as a welder's rod.

These rods can be purchased at any local welding supplies store. They come by the pound and in various sizes. The ones I like are 36 inches in length, 1/8th of an inch wide with a steel base and bronzed or coppered. Narrower ones are available but they become flimsy when pushed or hammered underground.

Tip: Ask the supplier for a heavy duty carrying case made of tough plastic. A couple of pounds of rods — perhaps 20 — in a cardboard case will shoot straight through the bottom.

It is critically important when using any dowsing tool to focus on the object of the search — in this case, a geopathic stress zone. You may decide to use this term although if you suspect or have been told other negative energies are present to broaden the scope. it is probably better to say: "I am searching for negative or toxic energy zones." You say whatever feels right and that produces beneficial results.

On arrival, the first move is to circumnavigate the exterior of the affected building. Start the scan at a particular point, such as a corner stone or a front door or a flight of steps, and then walk round the entire perimeter of the building with L-rods or pendulums in the search mode.

When you find a zone it is good strategy to mark it with a landscape flag. Colored landscape markers are normally purchased in 100 wraps at a local hardware store. Use one or both rods to discover the exact middle of the zone and place the marker.

If there is geopathic stress activity by the time you are finished the scan, you may have two or more markers decorating the perimeter. The reason for markers is they present a picture to the property owner where the zones are located. In addition, it saves time when breaker rods are placed.

Next you need to know the route or routes of the geopathic stress zone inside the building. This is mainly for the benefit of the inhabitants and will provide evidence for their discomfort or sickness. Use one L-rod in the indoor search mode and ask to show the location and route of the zone and follow where it indicates. Geopathic stress zones are based on underground streams and like streams on the surface, they do not travel in straight lines.

In this way you can track the inside route such as where people spend time such as the kitchen, dining room, office or study, sofas and armchairs to watch television or play games and always most importantly, the beds.

It is when you are dowsing in a home that the dowser should exercise caution not on what he or she finds but the comments that follow the discovery. At this point the dowser is on delicate and very sensitive ground.

The following dialogue actually occurred.

"Who sleeps here?"

"I do," she says.

"The zone runs across the top of the bed," I say. "How's your head?"

"I'm on pain killers — every day."

"Who sleeps there?"

"My husband," she says. "He doesn't believe in this sort of thing."

"The zone runs through his chest."

"He wakes up, heart racing, can't sleep. He's been to doctors and specialists — nobody knows what's wrong. When we go to the cabin he's fine," she says. "And so am I."

"How long have you lived here?"

"Two years. The health problems all started about a year ago."

"Geopathic zones work slowly. When you bought the place, did anyone mention bad energy in the house."

"We inherited it from my parents," she said, then shook her head. "They only had it five years. Mom went first with some form of brain cancer and dad followed her a week later with cardiac arrest. This was their bedroom."

"And nobody checked for anything under the bed?"

"I wanted to but my husband said I was nuts."

I resisted the urge to say: "If your parents had moved the bed to the other side of the room they might still be alive today." But I didn't because she had already deduced that and I sensed it was now starting to hurt deeply.

This is the dark side of being a geopathic stress hunter.

PHYSICALLY BREAKING THE ZONE

At this point it is time for the dowser to plant the breaker rods which will effectively deactivate the geopathic stress zone.

The breaker rods are placed directly across the toxic zone. The action should form a cross like this: +

Various dowsers have come up with different ways of placing the rods. The dowser places one in the ground where the zone enters the house or building and one where it leaves. Now here's the tricky bit.

Dowsing theorists say when you do this the toxic energy is beamed upwards at an angle of 63 degrees and comes down at 63 degrees. Now your strategy is to make sure the zone clears all of the upstairs rooms in the house or office. To accomplish this, the rods need to be placed a distance away from the house. This can be quite challenging because of trees and bush roots, lack of property space, etc. You may well have to go out onto the public sidewalk and plant a breaker rod in the space between the paving stones. This happens in built-up urban areas where houses do not have much yard or garden space.

If you cannot estimate or visualize an angle of 63 degrees, use a pendulum and ask: "Show me a YES response when I am standing in the right place to plant a breaker rod."

Once installed, you can check the zone from inside the breaker-rods coverage area. Use your L-rods to find the energy as it goes upwards. Depending where you stand the L-rods will cross at chest or head level.

Why the energy deflects at 63 degrees is a question long posed by dowsers and the answers have never been logically satisfying. One thing is for sure — it works! Another point: 63 degrees is a Cosmic number. It reduces to nine.

It is important to always remember to bury the breaker rods in the grass, lawn, dirt, garden so that they cannot be disturbed or found again. Why should the rods be hidden? Well, all sorts of things can upset your life-saving work. Some well intended gardener doing some work in the yard, a kid spotting the golden end pulls it up, or a weird person who detests or rejects the work and philosophy of dowsers secretly pulls them up. A number of women have reported that their husbands actually went out and tore up the rods after the dowser departed. One woman in northern New York said her dog went and dug them up.

But sometimes men can be quite devious. A sixty-year old lady on the verge of retiring had recently moved with her husband into an over-55 community and was now suffering cramps and aches. Would I come over? Watched by both the wife and her husband, I dowsed a geopathic stress zone, not under her bed, but passing through her study where she spent many hours writing poetry.

Two days later she called. "As soon as you had gone my husband went out and pulled up the rods in the ground. Luckily, he is away all week on business, so could you come over and place some new rods. He's like that. He doesn't like my poetry either. He says I'm as crazy as a coot."

BASEMENTS AND CELLARS UNPROTECTED

Now here is a problem. While breaker rods appear to interrupt and safely beam up the geopathic stress zone at an angle of 63 degrees above the building, they do not project or protect downwards. A logical argument for this is that Earth energy, beneficial or toxic only travels out or upward.

In other words underground basements, cellars, offices, bedrooms where people might spend time sleeping, working or watching television in basement recreation rooms, are not covered. They are still exposed to the toxic energy of a geopathic stress zone.

The dowsing solution: In the basement dowse the geopathic zone where it enters and departs. Yes, it will still be there although you have cleared upstairs. Check to see if it passes through a critical region — beds, sofas, armchairs, dining areas and office seats. If possible have key furniture moved to safe spots.

Next ideally clear the zone by placing a rod at each of the zone's entry and exit points in the basement or cellar. Tuck breaker rods under wainscoting, carpeting or even cracks in the floor. The dowser is now able to show the affected and cleared areas in the basement.

Will the energy affect upstairs again? Apparently not. It will be picked up and carried to safety by the rods protecting the main floor. Play it safe and check your work by going to the ground floor or even upstairs and checking for negative energy coming from the basement. Theorists have spent many a day trying to figure how these things work. My thoughts are: If it works why screw things up with theories.

CHECK THE HOUSE IS CLEAR

The job is not yet over. Enter the house and check that the house is clear. Demonstrate to the home or office people with L-rods and pendulums that the negative energies are no longer present — anywhere.

Dowsing with the techniques shown so far in this book are relatively simple and traditional and can be learned and used by anyone dedicated to work in this healing modality. All you have to do is practice and keep on practicing by performing the art of dowsing. It is many years since I heard the Welsh voice of my mentor Tom Passey, but it still echoes in my mind. "Practice! Practice! Practice! Then when you have done that, practice again."

Tom was so in tune with water and geopathic stress zones he knew when he was standing on one because he felt distinctly nauseous. Many dowsers holding L-rods can "feel" the presence of water and harmful energy zones just before the L-rods cross on target. It's called precognition. As one progresses in practicing dowsing you may find your own natural sensitivities emerging.

THE PUSHING-PULLING WATER PHENOMENON

Before installing and diverting the geopathic stress zone it is useful to dowse which way the water is flowing. Direction of flow is often important to a person sleeping full length on the zone and can explain different discomforts or pains.

If the subterranean water flow is from head to toe the body will suffer a "pulling" or a "pushing" sensation. The head will feel vacant and dizzy and the feet will feel heavy and swollen.

If the water flow is feet to head under the resting body, the blood will be drained from the feet and gather in the head and upper parts of the body resulting in weak and cramped legs and feet and a heavy swollen head, headaches, and general discomforts.

During half a century of investigative dowsing, Adolph Flachenegger discovered that 'pushing water' can cause headaches, blood congestion in and around the brain, severe nightmares, depression which could often lead to suicide. Such sufferers also experience cramps in their feet and legs and a general numbness in the lower limbs.

The "pulling water" frequently causes lack of balance, dizziness, blacking out, and even fainting. Such sufferers also feel heavy feet along with swollen ankles and legs.

These conditions have been observed by many dowsers including myself. The key to look for is when a person approaches for help they say "I wake up frequently and my head feels swollen and headachy," or "My head feels vacant and dizzy and my feet are glued to the floor." (Both actual statements)

It happens to both men and women. But men will not tell you, they will tell their partners who will relay information to you. The male of the species is not strong when it comes to weakness and suffering pain.

Clearing of the geopathic stress zones can bring relief and the body should start to heal.

DEEPER VEINS ARE MORE POWERFUL

It has been observed by many veteran dowsers that zones caused by deep running water have more powerful effects on the human body than shallow or surface water streams.

Most veins are found below the surface between 20 to 300 feet but they can be discovered at depths of up to 1,200 feet or more, especially when flowing through strata or sedimentary rock formations. The widths of the veins will normally range from nine to 18 inches but we have found subterranean streams up to 36 inches under houses, which have been either abandoned or torn down. Deeper flows appear to produce stronger affects at ground level and can be felt easily by pedestrians if they stand still for half a minute.

Shallower veins, often found in clay, are not so easily noticed which is why a person buying or renting an affected home will not notice a change in sleeping or living habits for several months, sometimes a year.

One key factor that alters the strength and effectiveness of a geopathic stress zone is the width. An 11 or 12 inch vein appears to be standard but veins measuring 20 to 30 inches or more in width carry a much more intensified geopathic stress zone as we discovered in an investigative project conducted in Mount Holly, New Jersey in the spring of 2018.

CASE: JAIME AND THE DEADLY BEDROOM

There are dowsers, hypnotherapists and folks who talk and listen to loved ones in spirit on the Other Side, the Astral World or Heaven. Occasionally you will find all three wrapped under one hat and that's mine. This unusual encounter comes from an earlier book of mine — "Insights" which talks of healing paths but it fits nicely in the purpose of this book.

The dowsing path can become littered with stories that should not have happened. One involved a young mother. We will call her Jaime. She possessed a frail body under a mop of withering white hair.

At 33-years-of-age she had a studious youngster aged eight. She also had a husband, Steve, an accountant, who might have better used his bulky body as a bouncer at a nightclub. In his younger years he had been a military policeman, a perfect disciplinarian who toed an unbending line when it came to altered states of consciousness and healing.

Jaime, battling cancer, was close to being treated with chemotherapy.

"You're a hypnotherapist," she said. *"I've heard that imagery can be a vital force in fighting cancer."* She declared her thoughts simply and factually in a calm voice. You did not have to be an intuitive to sense a desperate plea for help.

In the course of our initial consultation, she explained she had quit being a teacher to be an at-home mom, and to care for a sick mother. The family lived in a large Tudor-style home perched on a plateau in the beautiful mountains of West Vancouver, British Columbia. Tears welled up in her eyes as she revealed her mother had died four years before.

"She had cancer too. We actually moved into her house so we could look after her. She bequeathed the house to us."

Immediately an alarm bell sounded in my head. I felt the presence of a spirit, no, two spirits! One was Chang my healing guide, the other was an entity appearing as a thin elderly man covered in ugly skin blemishes. He wore heavy framed spectacles and: *"I'm Harry. Tell her to move the bed. Please tell her."*

"Jaime, who was Harry?"

Jaime was startled. *"My dad. Why?"*

"He's here." Balding, horn-rimmed spectacles, wears two wedding rings.

Jaime smiled briefly. *"He married mum twice."*

"What's the problem with the bed?"

"Nothing," she shrugged. *"When mum died, we renovated the room and I sleep there. My husband sleeps at the other end of the house. We don't see eye to eye."* She shrugged helplessly. *"Why do you ask about the bed?"*

"Dad says he slept with your mother in that bed"

"Yes! That's right"

"And they both died of cancer, and now you have it too," I said gently. *"I would like to see your home, if I may."*

Within the hour we were standing in the garden of the Tudor-style house perched on a rock plateau. Her bedroom window was above. I used my L-rods and found a band of negative energy coming through the rocks and passing right underneath her bedroom.

Upstairs in the room, the L-rods confirmed a strong geopathic zone of negative energy was running through the upper part of the bed, and anyone sleeping in the bed over a period of time, perhaps a year or two, would have a reduced immune system and suffer sickness. Dowsers have long called them *"cancer beds."*

"We can bounce the energy out of here by placing two breaker rods in the garden, one each on either side of the house," I explained. *"That's the root cause of your physical problem."*

We moved downstairs into the garden and I was taking two 36-inch copper breaker rods from the trunk of my car, when a Jeep careened up the driveway. Steve, Jaime's husband arrived with a black thundercloud face. Steve pushed a protesting Jaime inside the house and reappeared a couple of minutes later.

"I told her I didn't want my wife seeing any wacky hypnotherapist. We are Christians and your sort of people work for the devil. So would you please get off our property, or I will call the police."

Steve did not realize it, but he was committing his wife to a death sentence. I reluctantly departed as requested. That afternoon, Jaime came for a series of discreet hypnosis sessions for imagery and later that week started her chemotherapy. She did ask what she could do about her bed.

"We do have a visitors room. I will sleep there."

My pendulum and Chang confirmed its safety.

Several months later, she came in with good news. *"My doctors say I'm clear. Thanks for your help in getting me out of that terrible bedroom,"* she said with a pleasant smile, then hesitated. *"Why was Steve so adamant against having you help us?"*

Shrugging, I told her that many men have serious blocks about anything their ego is not trained to hear. *"That's why there are more women leading the way in metaphysics, spiritual development and healing,"* I added.

"Just as a footnote, Steve's gone. He couldn't stand the stress of my being sick," she said. *"So could you come over tomorrow and clear the house. I'd like to think that mum and dad's bedroom is quite safe. I'm sure they would like it that way."*

The shimmering image of the man with the horn-rimmed spectacles and the two wedding rings smiled behind Jaime. *"Your dad's giving you a thumbs up,"* I said.

She laughed happily. *"That's my dad. He did that whenever he was happy,"* she said, and then called out: *"Dad, thanks for letting us know. I love you. You know that. Tell Mum too."*

9

MYSTERIOUS ASPECTS OF GEOPATHIC STRESS

The original title for this chapter was "The Hidden Accident Tripper" but while it is real it sounded flippant, almost comical for a situation that is grotesquely real. Posing as monsters under the bed or in the closet is one thing, but geopathic stress zones are seemingly devious and often lurk in other places, in fact they can be so hidden away that we may be inclined to blame our own clumsiness.

Several years ago while Betty Lou and I were living in a cottage in Chaumont in northern New York. Our bedroom was upstairs and to get downstairs there was a flight of ordinary looking stairs much like an L-rod with an elbow turn.

Early one wintry morning I started to go downstairs and at the elbow turn something seemed to hold my legs for a brief moment, not even a second. It was at that moment I felt myself falling. I landed on my side and my left shoulder sustained injuries that took several months and an efficient chiropractor to heal.

I put it down to "not thinking" or "general clumsiness" and never thought it could be anything else.

Some months later I was carrying books downstairs and again felt a sudden and brief loss of control but managed to prevent a fall. A friend suggested the last step before the turn in the stairs might be out of sync with the others. It was not.

On the landing above the stairs, slept our two Chihuahuas in a large cage. One day Betty Lou noticed they were sleeping at the front of the cage and never at the back.

Geopathic stress zone? Dowsing showed a sneaky geopathic stress zone cutting through the corner of the house. It not only cut through the corner of the dog's cage, but it was directly above the elbow turn of the stairs. Outside the cottage in the lawn I placed breaker rods and bounced the toxic energy over the building.

Later, a lady who helped with domestic cleaning said she suffered a falling experience at the corner of our stairs. "It just happened. I was momentarily out of control."

Coral, a lady who has a townhouse in New Jersey said her husband, an active salesman, broke his neck while either sleepwalking or going to the bathroom. She said it looked as if "he had fallen down the stairs, but he was nowhere near the stairs when he was found."

A dowsing survey of the house showed a geopathic stress zone within inches of where her husband had fallen. Two years later he is still a quadriplegic.

Various people have told similar stories happening down hallways, passages and even paths in the yard — a momentary loss of consciousness. Now, suppose you were in a motor vehicle driving? We asked the question overseas and found a lot of answers.

A MOMENTARY LOSS OF CONSCIOUSNESS?

Some call it compressed body reflexes, loss of situational awareness, momentary loss of consciousness. It can be tripping over seemingly nothing, yet evidence is coming in towards breaking bones, cars and crashes at killer intersections or even railway disasters. In some cases if the driver does not possess a firm grip on the steering wheel, an invisible power may send the car hurtling off the road. It has happened. Let's take a look.

Expressways are the highest class of roads in India's road network. They are six or eight-lane controlled-access highways where entrance and exit is permitted by the use of slip roads. Currently at the time of writing there are 1,455.4 km (900 miles) of expressways operational in India. Pune, formerly spelled Poona under the British (1857–1978), is the second largest city in the Indian state of Maharashtra, after Mumbai. It is the ninth most populous city in the country with an estimated population of 3.13 million and is often referred to as the "Oxford of the East" because of its universities and colleges.

One stretch of the ninety-mile Expressway between Pune and Mumbai has witnessed 475 accidents in which 105 people died. According to scientists at the University of Pune: geopathic stress zones!

India's English language Daily News and Analysis which serves Mumbai, Ahmedabad, Pune, Jaipur, Bengaluru and Indore in a report September 3rd 2013 stated: "Experts list 7 stress zones on the E-way that affect drivers' reflexes leading to critical errors by them. Rise in the number of E-way accidents? Blame it, at least partially, on the geopathic stress."

Rajesh Rao writes: "At least that's what a survey and research of accident-prone spots on the Pune-Mumbai Expressway carried out by a city-based research academy shows. These spots, the research says, are located in geopathic stress zones that exert debilitating impact on the physiological condition of the drivers leading to critical errors while driving."

The report goes on: "After a careful study using scientific devices, architect Mayank Barjatya and his research team at Vastuworld Academy have identified seven accident-prone spots on the expressway, where a number of accidents have frequently taken place since the stretch was open for traffic," said the report. "The alarming rate of accidents on the expressway had prompted the academy to conduct a fresh survey of accident-prone spots.

"While human error is a major causative factor in these accidents, a question worth exploring is whether there could be hidden factors causing the human errors on high speed roads," said Barjatya.

Geopathy expert from Mumbai, Jiten Pandya affirmed that these geopathic stress zones on roads can compress body reflexes of a driver driving at more than 100 km per hour speed. (60 mph) When body reflexes are compressed there can be momentary or prolonged lapses of consciousness.

GEOPATHIC STRESS PROLONGS REACTION TIME

Avinash G. Kharat, a professor at Pune University studied the effect of geopathic stress on the reaction time of drivers. He specifically designed the SRTM (Simple Reaction Time Meter) to record the reaction time of drivers. "Continuous signals from our brain control our body and enable it to function correctly all the time. Concentrated geopathic stress blots out these signals so strongly that the flow of information to cells, glands and organs is more or less stopped and the reaction time of drivers increases," he reported. "Because of this increase in the reaction time of the drivers, accidents occur." The report noted distinct increases in blood pressure and heart rate when drivers were in geopathic stress zones.

Readers will note that the research teams used "scientific devices," but another team comprising geologists, engineers, environmental scientists from academies, colleges and the university at Pune, confirmed the earlier report but they used not only geo-resistivity meters but dowsers as well.

In a report to the International Journal of Modern Engineering Research the group submitted "Use of Dowsing and Geo-Resistivity meters for Detection of Geopathic Stress Zones."

The report said in part: "Geopathic stress (GS) is a natural phenomenon which affects certain places and can be damaging to human health," and added "researchers offer science based explanations about detection of geopathic stress zone by studying possible influences of geopathic stress on the human body."

They suggest "it somehow interferes with brain function and affects the release of melatonin, a hormone with particular importance for the immune system." The report adds: "An extensive survey was carried out and about 20 geopathic stress zone locations were identified using the dowsing method and with geophysical vertical electrical resistivity survey, in residential, commercial and transport routes like state and national highways in and around Pune city."

The report concluded by stating: "From the comparative study of resistivity technique and L-rod dowsing, we can authenticate dowsing. The authenticity of dowsing will help us in the investigation of Geopathic stress." In congested building areas, dowsing is a "faster method and can be used in built-up structures where the resistivity technique cannot be used."

Geo-resistivity Units are cumbersome, expensive and far from mobile. They are very accurate at in-depth soil and rock reporting of geopathic stress. Dowsers on the other hand are extremely mobile. They can walk, dowse and report in a very short time. Pune University appears to have the benefit of both.

Incidentally, the correct name is Savitribai Phule Pune University in Pune, western India. Founded in 1949 it is spread over a 411 acre campus and is home to 43 academic departments.

An interesting note comes from the Daily News and Analysis newspaper which quotes a practicing structural engineer in Pune city as saying that geopathic studies are not considered while constructing roads in India. That raises the question, does any country study geopathic stress dangers when building highways?

GERMANY: CARS GO OFF THE ROAD

Today it is known as European Route E75 but in the days of post-war Germany it was called National Road 75 and stretched from Hamburg to Bremen. It possessed an evil reputation, particularly at kilometer stone 7.5 where car drivers referred to it as the "death spot at Tostedt."

In his 1956 book "Harmful Radiations and Their Elimination" Bruce Copen tells of a British Army officer killed on the spot after his car collided with a tree. The highway, totally straight and asphalted appeared perfect. Since the British officer's crash dozens of similar accidents occurred, so much so that August Wrede, the police chief in Lüneberg took it upon himself to study the problem. He possessed one qualifying asset — he was a dowser with 27 years experience.

At the Tostedt death spot his dowsing rods reacted so strongly that he could hardly hold them. He discovered a geopathic stress zone crossing the highway. Shortly after, a group of police officers, journalists and the local government surveyors accompanied the police chief to Tostedt. Author Copen wrote: "The results of their investigations were convincing, almost sensational."

The group debated the question: Are the death rays strong enough to influence the driver or the car — or both? To answer the question it was finally decided to slowly run a car over the death spot — without the driver steering. The government surveyor and a police officer sat in the car. To everyone's stupefaction the car swerved from its projected highway line and ran towards the line of trees at the side of the road — the exact spot that Wrede had dowsed and marked before.

This experiment was repeated several times with others seated in the car, and still, the same thing happened. The car deviated from its course at the suspected spot and ran in the direction of the suspected stream — the geopathic stress zone.

In spite of the experiments, bureaucracy turned a blind eye. They said accidents along National Road 75 were fairly evenly distributed along the whole stretch. Still, the death spot at Tostedt remained and in three years, 19 cars and seven motorcycle accidents were reported there.

Sara O. Marberry in her 1995 book "Innovations in Healthcare Design" says: Researchers, noting that high-accident areas on the German autobahn also contained geopathic stress zones, installed special interrupter-type field devices to change the energetic environment and the areas no longer cause problems.

An interesting note comes from adjoining Austria: In 2003, Druids were recruited by Austrian motorway authorities as a last resort to address a notorious accident spot on the autobahn. As a result of their success in reducing the number of fatalities from an average of six per year to zero at the site, they have since been employed to address other black spots across the country (Leidig, CEN 2003).

NORTH AMERICAN HIGH ACCIDENT SPOTS

Americans are generally impervious to what goes on in the rest of the world principally because United States news media is addicted to — as one observer notes — "navel gazing". If Americans don't know about it, it does not exist. Hence most Americans have absolutely no idea of geopathic stress zones and dowsing.

Elizabeth is the fourth largest city in New Jersey. It is a transportation hub for land, sea and air and according to Time magazine it contains an intersection that is the "most dangerous in the state" and one of the most dangerous in the country.

The intersection is where US Route 9 meets with East Jersey Street in Elizabeth and is a joint responsibility between the City and the Federal Government.

In the article Time says it analyzed data from the National Highway Traffic Safety Administration and looked at a 10-year period spanning from 2003 to 2012. The analysis found the most dangerous intersection to be in Bensalem, Pennsylvania. But there were 11 runner-ups, each listed with six deadly accidents. The Elizabeth intersection listed as US Route 9 with Spring and East Jersey streets was named one of the 11 dangerous intersections. (See PHOTOS #6 on page 110.)

Spring Street feeds into Route 9 a few yards south of the intersection. It was the only crossing in the region that made the list. Incidentally Route 9 is paired with US Route 1 at this intersection.

As dowsers, we decided to investigate. A scan on Google Earth was stunning. Vehicle drivers on East Jersey traversing the intersection have to pass through three geopathic stress zones while north and south bound vehicle drivers have to pass through two. Yet in reality there are only two geopathic stress zones impacting the intersection but they branch into five affecting the entire intersection. In depth, one is 97 feet below the surface, the other is 180 feet.

The Bensalem, PA intersection at Knights and Street roads contains two geopathic stress zones which weave their routes back and forth across all roads. Straight through drivers cannot avoid crossing three geopathic stress zones. Statistics show seven fatal crashes here in 10 years.

The question that does not yet have an answer is did all or many of these fatal accidents result because the drivers unwittingly experienced "momentary lapses of consciousness" because he or she drove over several geopathic stress zones?

PERSONAL BLACK-OUTS

Thinking back, it happened in the fall of 2017. It was just after midday and I was driving home from a Spanish Conversation meeting. Driving along Rancocas Road I spotted the red light at the Mount Holly Bypass. I was first in line in the middle lane.

Suddenly, I felt overwhelmingly sleepy. I slapped my face to bring me to full alertness. The light changed a few seconds later. I drove home absolutely puzzled that I had stopped myself from dozing off. It had never happened before.

While researching and writing the above pieces on Elizabeth and Bensalem — the thought struck me: Does a geopathic stress zone cross the Rancocas Road right at the intersection. Google Earth and a pendulum readily confirmed my suspicion. A zone crosses all lanes of the road. It could affect first drivers in all three lanes east bound and two lanes west bound. It was two days before Christmas and raining but I wanted to confirm my findings on Google now in the physical. On the site, the dowsing rods confirmed the existence and even as I stood on the side of the road, I felt a weird pulling sensation in my legs. Toxic energy!

Worried? No, overjoyed! Now I could get some government people to see that threats to safe driving can come from below the Earth's surface.

Then it happened again: a momentary loss of consciousness.

CONFUSION AT SHAMONG

A local newspaper caught our attention. "Three accidents within five days at a Shamong Township intersection have left five people injured," said the New Jersey newspaper with a picture of a three-vehicle pileup.

The local fire chief described its as a "major accident," and added: "A Caravan hit a pick-up truck belonging to a lawn service and that pickup truck landed on another pickup.

What made it a "major accident" is that the lawn-service vehicle was carrying pesticides and the Burlington County Hazmat inspector had to check the scene, but everything was in order.

The 450-word story intrigued our dowser's mind. The intersection was Willow Grove Road which has stop signs while Stokes Road is also County Route 541 with no stop signs.

A scan on Google Earth revealed an intersection laced with geopathic stress zones. Through traffic on Stokes would have to pass through two while vehicles on Willow Grove, obeying the stop signs, would have to pass through six, all within a 125 yard radius of the intersection.

A lady living nearby told us: "It's hazardous! We hear crashes just about every other day. One day a car just left the highway and crashed into our house." We observed that it occurred exactly where one of the geopathic stress zones existed.

The Shamong Township Municipal Building happens to sit on one of the corners of this intersection. In fact one of the geopathic stress zones passes through the building. Betty Lou and I delivered a photo of the scanned intersection along with an article on geopathic stress to a clerk who answered our visit. She listened patiently and said the information would be "passed on".

We returned to our car and it was then the geopathic stress zones struck hard. As I drove onto Willow Grove, I felt extremely confused as to which way was home. I prodded the GPS for home in Pemberton, NJ and it showed the way.

"That's wrong," I said, now totally confused. "Home is that way." I drove 200 yards to get out of the geopathic stress field and then realized the GPS was right, so I did an about turn.

It was an experience I will never forget. The negative forces completely confused me not just for a moment, but for a couple of minutes. Even Betty Lou felt the confusion and said "We need to get out of here."

The bottom line is this: "As a dowser I work with Earth energies and know what affect they can impose on human consciousness. But how does an unsuspecting driver handle it? The idea makes one shudder to think."

We offered to clear the field of geopathic zones at Shamong, NJ as a public service but no one to date has given us permission. It is our golden rule, we do not change or heal energy anywhere without someone taking responsibility and saying "Clear it!" To date we have not heard from Shamong and confusion reigns.

CRASHING THROUGH THE ZONES

It is known as County Route 530. This little road stretches 2.7 miles between the end of State Highway Route 38 to the Hanover Street intersection in Pemberton, New Jersey. Every day this road caries an average of 25,000 vehicles heading east to such places as State Route 70 and the New Jersey shore, the huge Joint Armed Services Base of McGuire-Dix-Lakehurst, not to mention in the opposite direction, Philadelphia 30 miles away to the west.

In a $15.1 million improvement program the Department of Transportation says "Over the last ten years there have been twelve fatalities on this stretch of roadway. Crash data over the last five years documents 348 crashes in this segment, including 94 injury crashes." Government admits there is a problem.

On Google Earth we scanned the entire 2.7 miles in two sections. The first section showed twenty geopathic stress zones criss-crossing the highway in several clumps. The second section showed another ten, making thirty zones in all. Because CR 530 is reasonably close to our base, we physically dowsed most of the zones to confirm the Google Earth scans.

It is little wonder that people we know who travel the route, including ourselves, are always eager to get off CR 530.

My partner, Betty Lou Kishler then called the Department of Transportation Commissioner's office in Trenton NJ with the question: Does the N.J. Department of Transport have anyone studying geopathic stress zones in relation to highway accidents?"

The response from the front desk: "Send an email to the Commissioner's Correspondence Unit."

Enthused, we sent an email outlining geopathic stress and investigations that scientists in both India and Germany are studying "momentary loss of consciousness" on highways and using dowsers to detect the phenomenon. We explained how we dowsed and confirmed thirty geopathic stress zones existing across the CR-530 roadway and offered to meet department representatives either in their offices or on location at the roadway. Naturally, we offered to clear all thirty zones as a free Public Service. That was in early July 2018. At the time of going to print there has not been any response from any official on the CR 530 project which is now being expanded according to plan with the thirty geopathic stress zones still in place.

A LOSS OF SITUATIONAL AWARENESS ON A TRAIN?

On May 12, 2015 at 9:21 pm eastern daylight time, northbound Amtrak passenger train no. 188 derailed at MP 81.62 in the Port Richmond area of Philadelphia, Pennsylvania. It consisted of seven passenger cars and one locomotive.

The train had just entered the Frankford Junction curve at a speed of 106 mph where the speed is restricted to 50 mph. As the train entered the curve, the engineer applied the emergency brakes. Seconds later, the locomotive and all seven passenger cars derailed. Of the 250 passengers and eight Amtrak employees on board, eight passengers were killed and more than 200 others were transported to area hospitals. Amtrak damage was estimated to be in excess of $9.2 million. The weather at the time of the accident was 82°F with a westerly wind of 20 mph, with clear skies, and good visibility.

Two years later, almost to the day, Pennsylvania Municipal Court judge Thomas F. Gehret dismissed involuntary manslaughter charges brought against the Amtrak engineer driving the train. According to the Associated Press the judge said the crash was "more likely an accident than criminal negligence."

In a 2016 report, the National Transportation Safety Board said the driver accelerated the train when he did because he thought it was at a different section of the route "because of his loss of situational awareness."

"Loss of situational awareness"?

My mind reeled back to the reports from the engineers and dowsers at India's Pune University and my own experience at the traffic lights in Mount Holly. "Loss of situational awareness" and "momentary loss of consciousness"? Were they the same thing?

Working remotely at our home base, we brought up the location of the rail disaster — MP 81.62 near Philadelphia — on Google Earth and in the quarter to half a mile of track before the fatal crash dowsed the railroad for geopathic stress zones. When we had finished there were four almost equally spaced out over an estimated 460 yards. They ran directly across the tracks. (See PHOTOS #7 on page 110.)

Carrying a Google Earth picture of the scene and the zones we physically visited and dowsed the streets flanking the tracks and found the four geopathic stress zones exactly where we had dowsed them remotely. The next day we emailed our findings to the National Transportation Safety Board in Washington, DC.

We never received a reply.

This writer can only assume that the NTSB never examined the possibility of geopathic stress being involved in the accident. It is another indicator that American society is so geared to thinking comfortably inside the "box" that the very idea of a subterranean water vein triggering toxic energy rays which could cause a momentary loss of consciousness is "pure cookey" as one man said.

Yet the accidents are happening. About 20% of fatal auto accidents in the U.S. involve a "drowsy" driver, over 72,000 police-reported accidents in the U.S. involve "drowsy" drivers and 5,000 is the estimated number of people who died in drowsy-driving related motor vehicle crashes across the U.S. in 2016.

Is drowsy another name — a cover-up — for momentary loss of consciousness? Until U.S. scientists and engineers get out of their comfortable boxes and work open-mindedly in cooperation with dowsers on geopathic stress zones affecting highways we will never know. As we mentioned earlier, the German autobahn contained geopathic stress zones, by installing special interrupter-type field devices to change the energetic environments and the zones no longer cause problems.

10

THE TOOLS FOR MAP DOWSING

For years I always possessed an interest in map dowsing but somehow I did not fancy buying lots of maps and having a giant sized kitchen table to do the work. In younger years I enjoyed muddy boots dowsing, traipsing across landscapes with L-rods and pendulums to discover energy fields. As mentioned earlier, Google Earth appeared and changed almost everything.

It happened like this. One evening a creature named Bernard dropped by and with an overly polished Oxford accent suggested hunting for energy lines on Google Earth. "Start with the farm along the road," he said indicating a corn and soya producing area along a nearby road.

A dusty road heads off the main road to the farm and I brought up the place on Google Earth. Bernard suggested I use a pointer, a dried up ball-point pen, and move it slowly across the picture, making sure the focus was on finding geopathic zones. At the same time he instructed me to hold the pendulum away from the screen and watch it.

"Pay not any attention to the computer," he commanded.

With my left hand I could feel the pointer moving across the screen. Suddenly the pendulum started swinging clockwise, faster and faster and it finally started to slow.

"Move the pointer back until you feel the peak swing," he said, "then look at where your pointer is."

The pen pointed directly to the farm driveway where it exits the main road. One of the nice things about Google Earth is that the operator can enlarge the scene. This time I watched the pointer as the pendulum swung hard.

"Now record the coordinates," snapped Bernard quickly. The numbers appeared on the lower right hand side of the screen. I wrote them down.

Half an hour later I stopped the car outside the dusty road, looked at the GPS and the coordinates were spot on. Taking my L-rods I stood outside the car and the rods immediately crossed. The geopathic zone was running across the farm driveway as it starts from the main road.

Impressed with the achievement, I asked why I had to watch the pendulum and not the pointer on the screen. "That dear boy," came the reply, "is to ward off any bias that may be lurking in your conscious mind. Use it whenever you can."

Then it struck me: "Who or what is watching the pointer as it moves across the screen?"

"Oh, jolly good question! That's your Higher Self, your higher consciousness."

"Some people will say that's spooky," I said but there was no reply. Bernard had left.

During the winter months I searched for leys and nests of geospirals in various locations in upstate New York, Pennsylvania and New Jersey and elsewhere. Coordinates were systematically noted on large pads and when weather turned favorable Betty Lou and I embarked on a series of trips to physically check the energies. While the results were very good, we learned a lot too. Google Earth, the dowser's eye in the sky, makes work incredibly easy. I called it Armchair Dowsing and gathered enough ley line information to write "Chasing the Cosmic Principle: Dowsing from Pyramids to Back Yard America."

How we find cross country leys is also the way we find geopathic stress zones in homes, apartments, offices, factories, highways and railroads. How it started is something else.

REMOTE DOWSING AND DISTANCE HEALING

For a lot of years I was a member of the Muddy Boot Dowsers stomping through people's yards, fields, clearings always dowsing and clearing geopathic stress the hard way, planting breaker rods over geopathic stress zones.

The "remote" business all started at the 2017 annual national convention of the American Society of Dowsers where Betty Lou and I had a vendor's table. While I was away making a presentation a lady, Nancy by name, came up and thrust a $100 note into Betty Lou's hands and said: "Have Robert clear my home." So saying, Nancy disappeared.

The incident took me by surprise and I sat there stunned. While I recall Tom Passey using a decree system — Job's Decree he called it, I had never considered using it at least remotely. Yet I recall how Tom decreed there should be rain on a drought-plagued island off Vancouver Island and it rained for four days before someone called and asked him to stop it. "I can get it going," he said, "but I can't stop it." However, it did stop the next day.

Tom never shared the Cosmic body to whom he addressed the decree nor did he share the words he used. He was a man of few words and I sensed he worked mentally which is just as effective. Over the years I learned to perform hands-on healing as well as distant healing but rarely did I hear back from recipients. One must remember these were the days before email and texting.

Many dowsers who are healers are known to work at a distance on people suffering various sicknesses and I am sure it works. This is nothing new.

There are excellent examples of remote healing given by Jesus in the New Testament. The teacher was in Cana in Galilee and the dying son was stricken with fever in Capernaum, a distance of 38 kilometers or about 24 miles away. This event is reported in John 4:43-54 (NIV). Another remote healing is reported in Matthew 8:5-13 (NIV)

Distance healing techniques surface by many names. They include spiritual healing, intercessory prayer, auric healing, energy healing, shamanic healing, Therapeutic Touch, Quantum Touch, Qigong, Reconnective Healing, plus good old fashioned healing prayers offered up daily by millions of people.

All of these techniques are performed at a distance, perhaps a few feet to thousands of miles on the other side of the globe. Distance to these healers is not a limiting factor. What makes them all controversial is they do not match classical physical assumptions or fit within the belief systems of the average human being, mainly the skeptical male of the species. Women are more likely to become healers or resort to some of the healing practices mentioned above than men.

Back at base in Pemberton NJ I brought up Nancy's home in one of the coastal states and now had the problem of creating a decree. Enjoying a gift of writing, I wrote down some words. Being a mystic by nature, my belief is in a higher power, a Cosmic Force in the Universe, or perhaps an Infinite Intelligence as the Spiritualists say. Somehow the words "Holy Spirit" appeared logical on my laptop. So I addressed the decree: "In the name of the Holy Spirit I decree that the geopathic stress zone crossing this property be transmuted and converted into that which is good and beautiful..."

The "transmuted and converted into that which is good and beautiful" was a phrase used by Tom Passey and it always scored successes for him. Still, my creative mind later restructured the decree making it more of an intense prayer, but the first one worked anyway.

The geopathic stress zone hundreds of miles away in Vermont was clear. It seemed that remote clearing works. As I later advised some students in Elmira N.Y. "when a decree works do not burst into joyful hysteria, paint the town red and proclaim other way-out expressions of joy, simply focus on the Cosmic Presence and say Thank you!"

The Decree System which I will explain shortly was, I believe improved as time and the clearings went on. Questions quickly arose such as "How does it work?" and "How does it work so fast?"

I say this because in the next part of this book we are going to discuss and learn the finding, plotting and neutralization of geopathic stress zones anywhere it the world. What's more the dowser can do it while sitting in a luxuriously padded armchair in the comfort of the home.

A kind soul questioned me: "Is this the end of muddy boots dowsing?"

"Always keep your options open," I said.

WORKING WITH THE HIGHER MIND

Spiritual people love the word "diviners" while down-to-earth workers simply say "I'm a dowser." In other words both dowsing and divining mean the same thing: searching for targets both visible and invisible.

Regardless, the searcher will use rods, pendulums, Y-shaped twigs and a faculty called Higher Consciousness. It is not some rare oddity that only so-called weirdos and saints possess, the fact is every human being regardless of race, color or creed, is equipped with a higher consciousness. Sadly most people have never been taught to use or rely on this wonderful faculty.

Like eyes, nose, ears, tongue, and feeling fingers, the Cosmic Power, the Creator gave us a brain along with at least three levels of awareness or consciousness.

There's your waking consciousness. This is the state of awareness that comes into being upon awakening, it makes general decisions, supposedly executive decisions until it is time for sleep when it conveniently shuts down and disappears. It is much like the captain on the bridge of a ship. He or she makes decisions on leaving port, route, speed and destination. The real work goes on below deck.

This is the realm of the Subconscious Mind which, like a crew, generally manages countless human functions all below deck and mostly away from the awareness of waking consciousness.

For instance you don't have to think about breathing or keeping your heart pumping? If you did, it is unlikely you would make it through the day. It is that simple. It is this Subconscious facility that remembers everything — good, bad and indifferent — from the time you were in the womb to now. It is the guardian of habits, good , bad and indifferent. Can't stop yourself eating sugar? Check in with the Subconscious Mind crew below deck.

In addition to the Waking and Subconscious minds, there is also the Higher Consciousness which can and does perform a mass of interesting and useful things, if one allows it.

Higher Consciousness looks after your powers of intuition, sixth sense, premonition, instincts, creativity, inspiration, innate knowledge and yes, those much aligned faculties — psychic and metaphysics. The list also includes dowsing.

With Higher Consciousness one can also tune in to Holy Spirit, the Cosmic Forces, the Creator, Infinite Intelligence and God.

A sage once said somewhere along the path that if you are not using your Higher Consciousness to enjoy your life, you are like a robot without a soul.

Higher Consciousness can be an asset if the dowser seeks to avoid bias from memories of earlier work. If the dowser slips on focus, slips on objectivity, the Subconscious Mind may and will offer a memory of one or more previous cases. For example you may suddenly think: "I have had several Y-shaped geopathic stress zones this is likely to be another." Such a thought coming up during a scan may deter accuracy because it is projected by the Subconscious and not the Higher Consciousness.

The secret? Tune in to the higher self and take what comes. It can be done in various and simplistic ways.

GETTING A VIEW OF WHAT'S BELOW

One technique that often helps prior to the actual scan, is for the dowser to focus on the target — in fact think one's self into the property — and ask the pendulum to show how many geopathic stress zones enter the property and how many exit the property.

One in and one out is easy. Normally it is a solitary vein running through. One coming in and two going out will probably yield a Y-shaped vein, and two in and two out will not only have two veins, but they may be tied together in an H-shaped formation.

If a dowser has a good focus on conducting a geopathic stress scan there is no need to check on the number of veins. Incidentally two veins coming in and two veins exiting does not mean an H-shaped configuration. The veins may be at different depths and separated by dozens of hundreds of feet of earth. This is why it is a good idea to check the depth of veins, the widths and the direction of flows.

Two veins joining creates no special phenomenon, but two veins crossing at different depths can create an intense "hot spot" for anyone living or spending time on it. That is why it is necessary when performing a Google Earth scan of a property to ask if there are any Hartmann crossing points. A negative crossing combined with double veins crossing at different depths are truly dangerous examples of Nature gone wrong. Luckily, they are rare but the dowser should always be on watch.

Geopathic Stress Zones can always be detected by using the Higher Consciousness. The accuracy is often quite stunning.

THE TOOLS FOR DISTANCE DOWSING

The difference between tools used by a dowser physically tracking down and eliminating geopathic stress zones is quite different from dowsing at a distance in Cyber space. (See PHOTOS #4 on page 109.)

First one needs a quiet but comfortable workroom, a large screen laptop (17 to 22 inches), the Google Earth Pro Program (free), a good email service for the transmission of JPEG photos, a comfortable pendulum (I use a brass toggle from an old electric lamp), a notebook, a pointer (this can be an old dried up ballpoint pen), and a pen or pencil.

In addition a simple "clearance list" is very useful. Mine is on Microsoft Word with the date, the name of the person and the actual address scanned, and the time to the minute. The time is useful if you enjoy receiving feedback from those you have helped.

Regarding JPEG photos it is advisable to name them with the client and the address and keep the photo in a picture file with the month and year. Combined with the clearance list and the photo file, a dowser can quickly open a case if required at a later date.

OFFERING YOUR SERVICES

Announcing your services: There are various "free" avenues for exposure. Develop a newsletter and email everyone you know and ask them to pass on the information to people in need of help. Create a website. Many are available free or for a small monthly sum. Mention your webpage in your Newsletter and on your business card. Business Card? Absolutely, it's a mortal sin to leave home without a business card.

Join Facebook, Twitter and various social outlets and talk about your services and geopathic stress. A website is valuable too and many are "free" or charge a nominal sum. Once upon a time one had to be a tech wizard and know HTML to create one. Now it is easy. If you do not possess an artistic ability, find someone to help. You will need to promote your website, places like Submit Express will do it for free. If you take part in workshops or appear at conventions, psychic fairs, healing displays, always carry a Sign-up sheet stating what services you are offering. The sign-up sheet has spaces (1) Full name (2) email address and (3) physical address of the property.

Incidentally, the best and probably the most ideal method of running a geopathic stress clean-up business is to get referrals. You may get them naturally from pleased clients, but there again, you should always ask. It pays.

Talking of remuneration. Never provide dowsing services for nothing. You will quickly become inundated with curiosity seekers and those you do help will question your accuracy and sincerity. People enjoy paying for first class service, especially when you have the ability to clean their house of a disease called geopathic stress. One method is to suggest a donation and I do maintain this on my website.

When you find a family virtually dysfunctional and their home is likely to be foreclosed, clear the place and suggest they give a donation when their status improves.

Enough about administration, let's return to the front line.

"HELP! THERE'S SOMETHING WRONG"

Geopathic stress zones are not fussy! They can maim and destroy everyone from plutocrats and nobles living in palaces to the newly wed couple living in a mobile home across the lane.

The calls will sound like "There's something wrong with my house," or "There's a ghost in my home," or "My kid claims there's a monster in the closet." Even if the client is a relative or some other freeloader, there are three things the dowser needs to acquire.

An accurate rendering of the client's name, his or her email address, and the location of the property, in other words the physical address.

Cell phones or "mobiles" as they say in Europe are notably inferior when trying to listen to names and addresses. Insist on working by email. It's blunt because it gets to the point. If you let clients call on the phone you may end up giving thirty minutes or more of free therapy or counseling because you will assuredly get every argument the client has on how he or she is suffering and the fact the doctor has no answers.

The benefits of working by email include clarity and there is a record of name, address and an email that actually works.

It is advisable to have a webpage or a write-up on services you offer for sick buildings, geophysical stress, toxic energy clearing, etc. If you take part in workshops or appear at conventions, psychic fairs, healing displays, always carry a sign-up sheet stating what you're offering. The sign-up sheet has spaces (1) Full name (2) email address and (3) physical address of the property.

When you have the details, you are ready to work.

WORKING WITH GOOGLE EARTH

Open Google Earth and in the little white box in the top left hand corner write the property address. Most of the time, the system will correctly display the address while you are still writing it. Click on Search and the globe will spin to the destination.

The address always appears superimposed on the picture, but sometimes the words are between buildings or on property adjoining the target house.

If the building is partially obscured by trees, there is a little figure on the top right hand corner, bring it down to the road outside. At this point a photo of the house appears. Search for a number on the mail box or the house to confirm the address. If there is any doubt that this is the property in question, take a photo by clicking on the Image icon on the top row of symbols. On the right of the "print" icon is the "Save Image" icon. This will give you an identification picture to send to the client. Your cover note should ask for confirmation of the property. Once it is received, you can move on.

Put yourself into dowsing mode which was described earlier and conduct a scan.

Focus on the object of the search: a geopathic stress zone. Now, hold a pendulum with your writing hand. Make sure you have a short chain for fast response and with your other hand, hold a pointer. Start at some obvious point such as a doorway, steps, the corner of a building and slowly move the pointer along the outline of the building. Maintain your focus. When the pendulum starts to respond wait until it swirls at maximum velocity. Use the pin tool and mark each time the pendulum indicates a zone.

When the circumference of the building is complete, dowse the interior, planting pins as you go.

The scan needs completion. Between "Tools" and "Help" you will find "Add". Open it up and click on "Path." You can decide how wide and what color your lines will be. When you are ready a little floating box appears. This is a neat pen. Place it on the starting pin and left click the mouse. It is at this point a path of "ink" appears and you draw the path of the GSZ. When you have reached the end, left click again and the marking process stops and switches to a line in the color chosen. White is standard. I like yellow — it's Cosmic.

Saving the photo. There is a line of icons running along the top of Google Earth. You need the one that says "Save image." Make sure the picture is exactly what you want, then save it. It will be a JPEG image which is good for just about anything — a slide show, printing a document, and in this case emailing your findings to the client, friend or whoever you find yourself dealing.

Along the way, use a pendulum to dowse for back-up information such as: subterranean water vein, clay, broken rock, minerals? Width? Depth? Permanent or seasonal? All this information is useful. It demonstrates to the client that you are an efficient professional. You may never end up in court, but to have such information may get you described as an "expert witness." I sense this is on the horizon. Because one day someone crippled by geopathic stress is going to come back to a realtor, construction boss or property owner and say: "You sold me a home knowing that it contained a geopathic stress zone and said nothing about it."

SENDING THE SCAN

The next step is to email the picture to the person requesting the scan. This enables them to match the geopathic stress zone to any afflictions that might exist in the family. Your message should include a request for "permission to clear" the house.

This is your protection should anyone challenge you, legally or otherwise, and state you should not have done it. Permission will come by email and you have it in print. There is a code, generally unwritten among dowsers, healers and energy workers that the owner of whatever is being healed, must grant permission to heal or clear before the action is taken. This prevents a liberal minded healer wandering around and casting healing prayers on everything they choose. A mystic will tell you "a person must accept responsibility for the healing they request." Permission also strengthens the healing prayer or decree.

So, you receive permission and move on to the clearing.

PHOTOS

FROM ALONG THE WAY

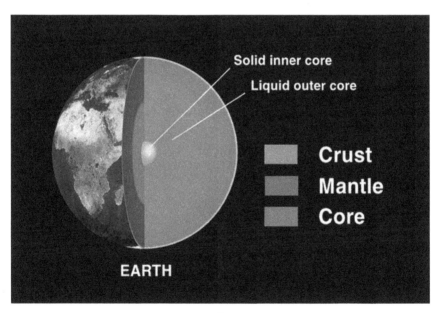

1

The center of the Earth, the core, has two parts. The solid, inner core is composed of iron which is surrounded by a liquid, outer core composed of a nickel-iron alloy. The two cores spin in opposite directions, making a natural dynamo and generating the Earth's magnetic field. Photo: NASA

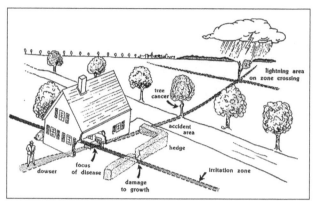

2

A famous illustration showing geopathic stress zones affecting a home, vegetation, trees and a dowser. Lightning often strikes geopathic stress points. The people in the house suffer reduced immune system protection before illness sets in. Illustration by dowser Dr. Joseph Kopp.

3

Twisted, bent and malformed trees are clearly symbols of the presence of geopathic stress zones. Dowser Betty Lou stops to give her Chihuahuas a treat. A tree gripped by the Silent Killer is at the side. Such malformed trees frequent the Rancocas forest area of New Jersey. Photo: Author.

4

For the Armchair Dowser working in cyberspace with Google Earth, a fairly large screen helps in accurately tracking any Earth energies such as leys, geo-spirals and geopathic stress. Here, the Metropolitan Museum of Art building along with parts of Central Park is shown in New York City as a demonstration. Photo: Google Earth / Author.

5

Police District 5 in Cincinnati was big news in 2017. The building was described as "sick" with allegations of cancer among the 34 staff members. Using Google Earth we dowsed the building to reveal two geopathic stress zones. In an email to the Commissioner we offered to clear them as a Public Service. No response. Credit: Google Earth/Author.

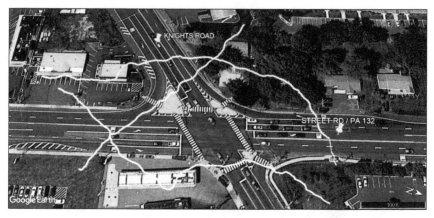

6

Described as the most dangerous intersection in the U.S., this is the Knights and Street roads intersection at Bensalem, PA. Dowsing shows three geopathic stress zones. Through traffic on either Street or Knights has to pass over three zones, all capable of causing "momentary lapses of consciousness". Google Earth/Author

7

May 12, 2015 , a northbound Amtrak passenger train was derailed in the Port Richmond area of Philadelphia, PA. Eight passengers were killed. The train was speeding. In 2016 the National Transportation Safety Board said the driver accelerated the train when he did because he thought it was at a different section of the route "because of his loss of situational awareness." Dowsed, the area before the crash shows four geopathic stress zones. An email to the NTSB brought no response. Credit: Google Earth/Author

8

This old tree with a refrigerator-sized burr on its trunk caught our eye. It stood alone on a freshly dug lot. Little did we know that the geopathic stress zone under the tree would lead us through half a mile of geopathic stress zones and a lot of unoccupied buildings. We were in for some surprises. Photo: Author

9

Surprise! Next to the big tree with the burr had been a house. Google Earth came up with a photo. Built in 1918 it would have been 100 years old this year. The geopathic stress created agony for the occupants who rarely stayed long. Look at the trees! All trying to avoid the house and the Silent Killer. Credit: Google Earth.

10

After researching and clearing the "Mount Holly Dead Zone" we relaxed at the St. Patrick's Day Parade in Fountain Square only to find another affected zone. This store had been a flower shop and two different restaurants all within a short time. The twisted tree on the sidewalk is the clue. We cleared that one too. The zone went also went through the Burlington County Offices. Photo: Author.

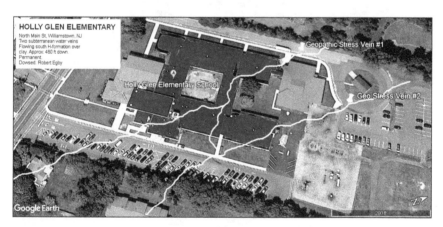

11

During 2017 regional newspapers carried stories about the Holly Glen School in Williamstown, NJ. It was declared "sick" with mold and ultimately closed for a year. Early on we dowsed the building and showed this scan on site to a maintenance engineer who told us "That's where the mold is exactly." We offered to clear it as a public service, but we never heard back. Credit: Google Earth/Author.

12

Meet Virtua's pride and joy, the full-service, state-of-the-art hospital at Voorhees, New Jersey. It contains 370 beds each in a private room, along with almost 700 doctors. It's called a "digital hospital." When Betty Lou visited the hospital, the author parked the car – right on a geopathic stress zone! Curious, we dowsed the building and found a string of geopathic stress zones. Credit: Google Earth

13

The author's dowsing scan of Virtua's Voorhees Hospital shows six white geopathic stress zones crossing the parking lots and the buildings. The Discovery Point at lower right is where the author parked the car and found the zone. An email letter was sent to the authorities along with a dowsing scan and an offer to clear as a public service. They actually replied and thanked us for the offer, but No! The offer still stands. Credit: Google Earth/Author

14

Imagine a house built on this land? It would be hell! This row of trees standing on almost a dozen geopathic stress zones lines is in the Veterans Memorial Park at Springfield Township, New Jersey. "Just to walk the path adjoining was difficult. Our feet felt so heavy," said Betty Lou. It's a place we often walk and as residents we gave ourselves permission to clear for all users, and of course the trees.

15

A clash of energies. This is at St. George's Anglican Cathedral at Kingston, Ontario, Canada. The photo was taken when we were tracking ley lines—old tracks as they are called. Here a ley line runs across the front steps of the building and it also passes through a tree suffering from geopathic stress, hence the twisted trunk. Photo: Author.

16

The relaxing and beneficial geospirals can be found in many historic places. When trees grow on one they experience accelerated growth, as the ones here at the Veterans Cemetery in Rosiere, New York. In the immediate area there are at least 19 geospirals making the area a vortex. Got an ache? Stop by and sit for 20 minutes. You'll be glad you did. Photo: Author.

11

THE DECREE: BASIC AND SUCCESSFUL WORDS

This is the nitty-gritty of clearing and we are including it now for those readers who are skilled in dowsing to move ahead. The philosophy and rational of this is described after this section.

To perform a complete clearing, prepare Google Earth and bring up the target on the screen. Make it so that the entire property is viewed. Make sure all your GSZ markers are visible. Then keep a pendulum and pointer handy. A pointer can be a dried-up ballpoint pen or a pencil — anything that will not leave a mark on your laptop screen.

PREPARATION: In order to process a decree it is necessary for the dowser to be in a light state of trance, the best is the Alpha State, a light meditative state. This can be done by closing one's eyes and imagining you are looking up to a blackboard inside your forehead. Hold that for a slow count of five to ten and then open one's eyes. This will induce a comfortable relaxing Alpha State.

FOCUS: It is necessary to focus on your target, in this case the home or property you wish to clear. One way of performing this is to hold a pendulum in your right hand allowing it to swing gently. Then with your left hand, hold the pointer over the target and make a movement slowly but firmly encircling the target. Note: If you are left-handed, reverse the process. Keep encircling the target and as you do, say in a strong voice: "In the name of the Holy Spirit....In the name of the Holy Spirit...."

You can use whatever Universal Power to what or home you subscribe. If you have trouble with names like God, the Creator, Infinite Intelligence, use Cosmic Forces. We have found all work just as well and that it is the Intent that works. Use whatever feels right for you—and works! Holy Spirit does not have an ego problem.

As you perform the encirclement, with your eyes on the target, your pendulum should start to swing vigorously. After about seven encirclements with the pointer the pendulum should be at peak. Relax the process and go into the decree.

> *In the name of the Holy Spirit.... We decree that all negative energy existing in this place including a geopathic stress zone — be transmuted and converted into all that is good and beautiful. We ask that this decree remain in existence for one hundred years from this date. (Or...until the end of time.) Amen.*

Additional notes: The above Decree works well even when lightly modified. It not only works remotely, it also transmutes and converts negative energy even when the dowser stands directly on top of it.

The decree should be said with marked enthusiasm. In your focused state you should be enthusiastic, fully confident that the process is working. The decree is in fact a focused prayer and all successful prayers need imagery and enthusiasm. Never allow the idea of failure to slip into your mind. As a great teacher once said: "Whatever you ask in prayer, believe you have received it and it shall be yours." That is key. There should be no hesitation in making the decree. Think it is happening. Think that it has happened.

You may well ask who is the "We decree" in the wording? I find that "We decree" gets away from the egotistical "I decree" and gives it strength. After all there are two elements working here, You and the Holy Spirit. It makes a lot of sense when dowsing to work as a team, and this is a good example.

"One hundred years"? We used to say "this decree is in force until the end of all time." My friend Bernard suggested a more finite time hence the century was included.

It is important to signify or command that this decree is permanent so ensure this by including the time element.

Do not be afraid to change the wording of the decree. I find that repeating phrases as you might hear in a song is helpful. Example: "be transmuted and converted...transmuted and converted..."

After a while you will develop your own style and discover what is best that works for you — the target — and the Universe.

You may find that the decree and clearing takes focus and energy so it is best to recall the message at Delphi "All things in moderation." In other words do not overload your system by doing several clearings in one day. I prefer to restrict it to one a day. If perhaps you feel exhausted or overwhelmed for a few seconds afterwards, this is normal. Take in a slow deep breath and as you breathe out say aloud: "Awake! Wide awake now!"

TRAINING AS AN ENERGY TRANSMUTER

Tom Passey, long time Canadian dowser and one time president of The Questers, the dowsing society based in British Columbia, taught me back in the late 1970s how to transmute energy and it never entered my mind that it could be done at a distance or remotely until early 2017. By distance , I mean on the other side of the planet!

Tom was one of the greatest dowsers one could ever hope to meet. He knew energy, worked with energy and he played it to the hilt. He was president of the Canadian Society of Questers. He was also my friend and colleague.

Quester is the Canadian term for dowser, and Tom was not only a great teacher and lecturer, he had a great personality and a tremendous following of students and admirers. He not only came over as a friendly grandfather, but as an ancient wizard in modern-day clothing. Some people thought of him as a reincarnated Merlin from Arthurian times in England. By coincidence, he was born and grew up in Wales.

Tom had an amazing understanding of energy and frequently told students attending workshops: *"All disease comes from blocked energy. The worst thing you can have in your body is stagnant energy."* In a healing workshop we did together on Whidbey Island, he looked at a woman seated in the front row and said: *"You have an energy block near the bottom of your spine, and it's been bothering you for months."*

The young woman nodded, and Tom asked her to come forward and sit on his chair. As she sat down, he waved his "wand." Most dowsers use pendulums when working closely on a subject, but Tom had a thin black fly-fishing rod that he carried everywhere. It would "talk" to him, in exactly the same manner as a pendulum talks with yes, no, can't say, don't know.

"You spend a lot of time crunched forward in a desk chair that's too tall, and it's impacting your back," he said. Her name was Annie and she nodded vigorously. *"I never thought of it that way,"* she said. *"It will be changed on Monday."*

"Okey dokey," said Tom. *"Are you ready to let go of the discomfort* (he never called it pain) *and be well?"*

120

"Oh, Yes! Yes! Yes!"

He tapped her back with his wand. *"It'll be gone at lunchtime."*

Sure enough, half way through lunch, Annie came rushing up to Tom, her eyes glistening with joy. "You'll never believe this Mr. Passey, it's gone! It's really gone."

MOVING WATER

Tom always enjoyed those moments of pure belief. He enjoyed healing, but he detested water. "It makes me nauseous," he said, which was ironical because he excelled in energizing and moving water.

A Shuswap Indian complained that his well had gone dry. Friends claimed it was the work of bad spirits. Tom looked down the well for a few minutes, then declared *"There's a nice little vein ten feet away. Will fifty gallons a day be enough?"* The Indian was hesitant to say anything, but finally nodded. Next day the Indian, all excited phoned Tom to tell him his well was full with sweet water.

We were in the Shuswap's Salmon Arm attending the Canadian dowsers convention. During a quiet moment, I quizzed Tom on how he got water to divert its course. "It's in the Bible, Bob. The prophet Job said: Thou shalt also decree a thing, and it shall be established unto thee: and the light shall shine upon thy ways." (KJV Job 22:28) He smiled softly. "When you are a dowser and you want to change something, you have to decree it. That's the secret. Remember that."

"Did you do that with Annie?"

Tom nodded. "Dowsing is the finding, decreeing is the order to the Cosmos for an action to be carried out. It's the same as ask and you shall receive. How many times does one have to be told?"

In workshops when the weather was too bad for students to venture outside, Tom would look at the floor and with his rod, a shortened fly-fishing rod, he would state: "I decree a line across this carpet six feet in length."

The students armed with pendulums or L-rods walked and searched back and forth to find it, and most did. Tom possessed tremendous patience.

As the workshop was coming to an end he would say: "Never leave a created energy line, positive or negative. Neutralize and clear it."

In my own workshops I repeated Tom's teachings and never once did it enter my mind that there existed a deeper side to clearing negative energy lines. It happened one day in the fall of 2016, a lady called, said she was sick, could not sleep very well and insisted she must have a geopathic stress zone running through the house. "Can you come over?"

Unable to visit because of commitments in New Jersey, I did take time on Google Earth to check her house some 20 miles away. Sure enough, a geopathic stress zone wound its way through her home. I emailed a photo showing the problem.

"That's where I try to sleep," she cried. "Could you please come out and put in the rods you are always talking about?"

Over her protests I said: "Leave it with me. I'll see what I can do."

As I sat back in deep thought, I'm sure I heard Tom's voice: "Bob, neutralize and clear it."

"She's twenty miles away."

"Use Job's decree," came the voice. "Bring her place up again on the computer screen."

In a few seconds the house was on Google Earth. "But that's not now," I pointed out. "It's a photograph probably years old."

"Do it! Don't look for excuses!"

For the next minute I focused on the house and the geopathic zone I had marked on the screen, then in a firm voice asked the Cosmic Forces "to transmute and convert this geopathic stress zone into energy that is good, beautiful and healthy." It was short and very much to the point. I wondered if it would work.

"Use a pendulum and dowse the line you have on the screen," said the voice.

"It's clear! It's gone," I muttered unable to believe.

The lady emailed me next day: "I've just had the best night's sleep I have had for years," she wrote, "Whatever you did, I am very thankful."

The incident triggered a host of memories from my days — ten years in fact — at the Vancouver Psychic Society where Isabel Corlett and Patrick Young, both mediums from the United Kingdom taught me not only the art and skills of hands-on-healing but also the ability to perform remote or distant healing as it was called — on people!

There are three aspects of performing tasks remotely: the ability to focus, the intent to heal, and knowing that the energy is there. It's like getting on a train or an escalator — you know it is there.

Various mystery schools over the centuries have taught the existence of energy currents that constantly sweep through the Universe, the stars, planets and our lives. Some people call it the Cosmic Forces because they are always in attendance. Some people call the energy currents of the Universe, Infinite Intelligence, others The Creator, or God, I prefer Holy Spirit.

You see, it's not just energy that is dominating or frequenting the Universe, it is an energy with intelligence that can and does communicate. Whatever name you might call it, one needs to recognize that energy as a higher and beneficial power, and just like a train or an escalator you have the ability to jump aboard and do something beneficial for yourself and the Universe.

If you wish to clear an energy zone, it is considered best that you practice first by creating one.

CREATING AND CLEARING "TEST" ENERGIES

It helps if the dower can relax, focus, image and have a belief that he or she can achieve spirit communication by talking with departed loved ones, spirit guides or saints and angels. It also helps if the dowser has a belief in some higher power we have mentioned earlier.

If you have all the above, start small, do not rush learning this process. Fast-track learning has a knack of blocking the inspired and in-a-hurry dowser. Here are some practical exercises that will help.

Exercise 1: Find an object such as a mat, a carpet or even a piece of wood several feet wide. Using a pencil or marker make a spot on one corner and another on another corner. Now pause and then say: "For demonstration purposes I decree that a two inch wide geopathic stress zone exists between these to points. It will be there for anyone to measure and feel as a negative energy strip. Amen."

Then pick up a pendulum or L-rod and check to see if it is there. Do not doubt its existence and you will find it. Then ask a friend to use a pendulum and find your "geopathic stress zone". If you have done it correctly, the line will be there for anyone to find. When you have finished the exercise, close with: "I decree this line has completed its work and can now be dissolved. Amen" Practice this until it works well for you and your dowsing companions.

Someone may ask: "Why did you create a negative energy line?" The answer is: "So that I and any students can feel a negative energy line." The logic is the more you get to know and feel negative energy the more effective you will be as a healer.

CLEARING A STRESSED TREE

Exercise 2: Using either L-rods or pendulum venture outside and find a bent mal-formed tree likely to be growing astride a geopathic stress zone.

Check the existence of the zone and place markers on either side of the tree — perhaps six to ten feet away from the tree. Have a dowsing partner to witness and confirm your findings. Your exercise is in fact a task to clear the tree of geopathic stress. When you are set, focus and work to identify with the tree and when ready address the geopathic stress zone and say:

> *"In the name of the Holy Spirit I decree that the negative energy, particularly the geopathic stress zone running through and affecting this tree, be transmuted and converted into all that is good and beautiful, and that all energy passing through and surrounding this tree is now and in the future, beneficial, healthy and uplifting. I ask that this decree be in force until the end of time. Amen."*

Immediately have your witness confirm your action with a pendulum or rod. If performed properly the tree should now be free of harmful negative energy. It happens just like that. There is no waiting for the clearing to happen. It became a fait accompli instantly, while you are stating the decree. So make sure you know what you are decreeing.

The wording of the decree can be changed to fit your needs. Stay rational. Make wording simple and to the point. Resist over-decorating with such flowery words as "Lord of all Angels" and "Infinite Helpers."

Exercise 3: Find someone you know, a friend, relative or colleague who has a geopathic stress zone running through their house. Test it to make sure it is there. Talk to them, ask questions regarding the problem, and get a feel for their situation. Take a photo of the house and go home. Quietly bring up the photo on your laptop and look at the house. Using a pendulum ask "Can I now decree this house free of negative energy? When the pendulum responds in the affirmative, state your decree."

"In the name of the Holy Spirit, we decree that all negative energies, particularly the geopathic stress zones affecting this house be transmuted and converted into all that is good and beautiful, and we also decree that from this moment forward all energies existing and entering this house be positive, healing and healthy, inspiring and uplifting. We also ask that this decree be in force for the next 100 years. Amen."

Let the people know that you have completed the clearing process. Tell them the exact time of completion and it is a good idea to maintain a journal or record.

You may notice that we have included an energy blessing from the original decree stated earlier. Specifically it reads: *we also decree that from this moment forward all energies existing and entering this house be positive, healing and healthy, inspiring and uplifting.* This also ensures that not only is the geopathic stress zone neutralized and restored to natural and beneficial Earth energy, but that all energies now and future will be beneficial. If you are going to clean a house or a building, you can polish it too.

Congratulations, you have just completed your first remote clearing of a geopathic stress zone. Now you are ready to work with Google Earth and clear any negative energy field on Earth. Yes! No kidding! It's as easy as flipping on a switch. Have confidence! Love dowsing, Love decrees and Love yourself for doing it.

GETTING OVER THE DISTANCE HURDLE

The next challenge or problem to jump over is the self-imposed limitation of distance. It can be daunting. The challenge came to me head on a couple of weeks after I had discovered my ability to clear houses down the road or in the next county. A couple of successes in upstate New York and Vermont all 300 miles away had been chalked up, but nothing major.

One day on Facebook's Messenger a teenager pleaded with me to dowse and rid the negative energy playing havoc with her family and relatives all gathered on a farming commune. There were four houses all within a few hundred yards of each other plus some barns and outhouses. "Everyone is angry," said the text. "They never talk with each other. If they do say anything it is bitter and full of hatred. Can you exorcise a bad spirit?"

On Google Earth the farm appeared but it was a hodgepodge of buildings and riddled with geopathic stress zones, so, using the tool on Google Earth Using the Tools a circle was drawn round the entire place. The farm was near the town of Brogo, New South Wales, Australia and some 12,000 miles away from our base.

A wave of hesitation struck me. "Don't worry about distance," said a spirit friend of mine. "Distance has no meaning. It's all in the mind. Go ahead." The girl gave the permission to clear so the decree for the farm was put into effect. Two days later an elated message came over: 'It's a miracle! Everyone is walking around smiling and talking to each other. It's lovely!"

That response opened the doors to us working on a global basis. Requests came in from Ireland, Italy, Belize, Australia, Canada and from various parts of the far flung United States, like San Diego and the West Coast.

For dowsers seeking to clear the world of geopathic stress zones there are two aspects to which one must adjust: Get comfortable in performing remote clearing at a distance and the fact that the clearing, the change of energy from negative to positive happens not slowly but faster than the blink of an eyelid. It is just as if the Cosmic Forces flicked a switch.

One habit I have adopted is to record the exact time the decree is made. It can be important for the client. "It's strange, my books never move, but a whole shelf moved and I glanced at the clock — 1:58 p.m. — the time you cleared my home."

Another lady near Milan, Italy: "I was sitting talking to a friend and we both noticed a strange but pleasant scent or perfume. It felt so fresh. We both checked the time and it was exactly the time you cleared our home."

One lady in Princeton, New Jersey in thanking us for the clearing, wrote: "We did hear unusual noises around and inside the house throughout the day yesterday. My husband commented several times that the wind was whistling outside with a sound we haven't heard here in the past — and he doesn't know anything about any of this. I heard new metallic sounds in the kitchen and different creaking sounds above our bedroom. All very intriguing!"

When you have achieved a measure of success, do not overreact, throw a party, scream it all over the social pages, simply accept it as another step on your spiritual path as a dowser and know that the Universe is with you.

ADVANTAGES OF REMOTE CLEARING

There are a number of distinct advantages for dowsers and clients using the remote clearing process of geopathic stress zones and similar toxic energies.

1: It is not labor intensive. The dowser does not have to travel, trudge through muddy yards, plant breaker rods, and sometimes wielding a heavy-duty hammer to get the breaker rods through weeds, roots or broken rocks. Also physical dowsing often requires the dowser to remove coats and muddy boots to check zones in bedrooms and lounges.

2. When the geopathic zone is "transmuted and converted into all that is good and beautiful" the entire toxic segment of the subterranean

water vein is neutralized, benefitting not only the client, but also any neighboring properties. Geopathic stress zones can run for quite a distance, sometimes the best part of a mile under neighboring properties.

3. It is done "instantly" and does not rely on the dowser to come and clear it at a mutually agreeable date.

4. If the client lives in an apartment, the geopathic stress zone will be affecting everybody below and all those above, even if there are forty or a hundred floors. By clearing a zone, every apartment above and below is cleared, the remote dowser's work has been shared by all. That's the difference between physically planting breaker-rods — that is space specific. Decreeing a neutralization of a geopathic stress zone is non-space specific. The dowser clears the entire route of the toxic zone. The one "permission" from a single client can benefit a neighborhood.

5. The detection and clearing by remote technique allows the dowser to "go to work" wearing pajamas and slippers. The armchair dowser is at liberty to choose hours of operation. However, some dowsers like myself, do appreciate the unpleasantness of living with a geopathic stress zone so we normally respond as soon as the request comes in.

Of course, our services in healing homes and buildings do not replace any client's consultation with a doctor. If one's health problems persist after a house healing, please head for your local health professional.

SOME REMOTE CATCHES

Many remote clearing and healing of homes work well, but there are some instances when plans go awry. This does not mean they are faulty, it does mean there are some catches and these even occur when clearing houses in the physical through the planting of break rods to divert toxic energy.

The first instance is when the home resident does not react to the clearing, in fact if there is any reaction it is against the change. Observations such as "There's been a change and I feel definitely worse," or "Yes, I feel it but I'm not happy."

It has been mentioned by dowsers and healing practitioners for many years that there are some people who become so acclimatized to living in a toxicity environment, like that produced by geopathic stress, that they actually expect the change or the cleansing to resemble the old way of living.

It has actually been found that people who have been living and suffering on a geopathic stress zone will find a new home with an identical environment — a geopathic stress zone running through it.

Then there are the people who have forgotten what it is like to live in a geopathically stressed free environment and may complain for days, even weeks that the change is slow in coming.

There are the people who believe that their toxic environment is the result of visits or residential stays by negative spirits. Now this phenomenon is distinctly possible. Some negative spirits from the lower levels of the Spirit World / Heaven / Afterlife / Astral Plains appear to enjoy basking in toxic energy and indeed watching unfortunate humans suffering in that state.

This is why it is important for remote cleansers to always check a home for negative entities and include their existence in the decree or prayers of cleansing.

IMPORTANCE OF TIME IN THE DECREE

Some people may consider that time is of little importance in issuing a decree but we did find it does matter. In the early days of remote dowsing and clearing by decree we omitted to state a time for the decree to be effective. After some months the same geopathic stress zones reappeared as toxic as ever in two homes.

When we started we included the words: And this decree shall be in effect "until the end of all time" and another was "until the end of the world." One hundred years is understandable because by 2118 some hi-tech person will have come up with a device that cleans up toxic energy world-wide. Time will tell how everything works out..

While the idea of dowsing from an armchair may appeal to some, it is far from being inactive, in fact it has led to my being even more active with an activity known as Investigative Dowsing. It was this that led us to major geopathic stress problem in the old town of Mount Holly, New Jersey.

12

DRIVING A WEDGE INTO
THE UNKNOWING

In the world of dowsers, there are two sorts. The majority are students, teachers, pendulum swingers, mini L-rods tucked away in a pocket book, Sunday class teachers, and occasional workshop leaders in everything above. There has to be room for pacifist dowsers and that is fine.

The other sort is the warrior, the advocate, activist, the dowser who is not afraid to face the authorities, property owners, realtors, city hall, confront their habitual ignorance of dowsing and Earth energies, and drive a wedge into a strange phenomenon, the American Pride of Unknowing. Included in these ranks is the Muddy Boots Dowser and an activity I call Investigative Dowsing. .

As you will realize many Americans bathe in total ignorance of geopathic stress, not because they want to, but because it is part of the culture. They do not want to know that there are Silent Killers under countless thousands, perhaps millions of beds in modern day America. Scientists, they say, do not acknowledge dowsing as a science, which as you will have learned is totally false. This book has shown that scientists have and are using dowsers combined with electronics in their research.

American media are notorious for navel gazing and ignoring what is happening overseas, particularly to Europe where scientists, ironically pay attention to what is going on in the United States. It was at the Institute for Frontier Questions of Life, an organization and website owned by University Professor Dr. Gerhard W. Hacker in Salzburg, Austria, that we found out that geopathic stress zones had actually been created in a United States laboratory. Where? New Mexico!

Aquifers ("stringy water ways") are probably the most common cause of geopathic stress: groundwater works its way through countless tiny pores. According to the principle of an "electro kinetic microchannel battery", frictional effects can lead to electric and magnetic fields that are superimposed on the Earth's magnetic field. Carried out by physicists, this hypothesis has been replicated in laboratory experiments, and their findings conclusively confirm the existence of this effect. (Ref.: Stephen R. Brown, Robert W. Haupt: Study of Electrokinetic Effects to Quantify Groundwater Flow. Sandia National Laboratories, New Mexico; Sandia-Report 1997).

To get the above information, all I had to do was write on Google Search "Geopathic stress studies Europe." That got me to Dr. Hacker's website and the news that happened in our own country. Amazing what the right question will do.

THE CHALLENGE OF PUBLIC SERVICE

Working with home owners is generally straight forward and easy. Once they know there's a geopathic stress zone running through the house, all they desire is for the dowser to clean it up. With affected business, it is a completely different situation and certainly not easy.

Trying to perform "Public Service" dowsing totally free can be enlightening as much as it is disparaging. However, it is a true learning experience in every way.

Commercial business, industry and government well recognize the phenomenon of a "sick building". When the situation occurs the owners readily announce they are seeking to improve air conditioning, better space for employees, improved staff relations, but nobody ever mentions earth energy or geopathic stress zones. That is a no-no, a forbidden subject in spite of the fact it is maiming and killing people as we will show.

United States health care spending in 2016 increased 4.3 percent to reach $3.3 trillion, or $10,348 per person in that year and it is growing. Two years before in 2014 it was $2.6 trillion. How much of this resulted from people getting sick from living and/or sleeping on geopathic stress zones? It's a red hot question but do not expect to get educated answers soon.

It is no longer sufficient for a dowser to clear a home of geopathic stress and proclaim the benefits of dowsing. The movement needs to make a noise, a substantiated noise and demonstrate what dowsing can do. Science is moving in its own quiet way but dowsers need to stand up and ask questions. This opens up the role of the Investigative Dowser.

The Investigative Dowser is not just an experienced diviner. When confronted with toxic energy zones s/he remembers the five Ws — Who? What? Where, Why? When?

This attitude will not get you into a fast, clean ride to fame, however it will take you on an arduous and perhaps enlightening research mission and produce powerful material you can use to promote dowsing and make people aware.

Bearing all this in mind, we became involved unwittingly in a case called "The Dead Zone in Mount Holly, New Jersey." Except for a few deserted buildings all has been reincarnated, born again whatever, but in the first months of 2018 the Silent Killer reigned supreme: the zone was virtually dead except for an actor — I really should say, an Artistic Director.

DISCOVERING A TOWN'S DEAD ZONE

Mount Holly is a township and the county seat of Burlington County as well as an eastern suburb of Philadelphia, which is across the Delaware River. On any given day about 10,000 people live and hang their hats here, watch tourists exploring the Old Mill Race Village which is a collection of quaint 19th century shops that peddle everything from Appalachian dulcimers, jewelry, crystal balls, pendulums, incense, scarves and T-shirts to ice-cream and donuts.

Rancocas Creek is a river with no singular identity: it snakes its way through the town on its way to the big river. Once upon a time Mount Holly was home to big industries and moguls who left their names on street signs.

When I first came to Mount Holly various people, some academically trained in nearby Princeton, would claim there is another "mysterious river" tucked away in the earth far below the Rancocas. They would add that those who know say it is "the domain of evil spirits" that occasionally come up to street level to haunt modern-day Mount Holly. This phenomenon is often mentioned in Halloween columns and by owners of the old curiosity shops.

One store owner who believed the dark side to the town exists, told Betty Lou that a "vortex exists and people who know, warn others — it can take you down!"

Anyone with good dowsing experience when listening to such points as "mysterious river" and "the domain of evil spirits" and "it can take you down" will know these signify the existence of geopathic stress.

The old Mill Race community had never been an attractive area for us. Several times over the years we would start to drive through its narrow old world streets and suddenly have a change of mind. We felt a fast need to take a right turn and drive out, but when a fascinating coffee shop

Breaking Grounds opened in a 1775 house on White Street, we decided to stop over and take a look.

As soon as we got out of the car, our feet started to feel heavy.

"Geopathic stress zone," said Betty Lou.

It spanned a parking lot, White Street and swept off between some buildings.

"That's why some people come by, then change directions and leave," I said. "It's the same as a geopathic stress zone across the driveway of a house up for sale."

There was no one to ask for permission to clear but as it was bothering our peace of mind, a decree was in order. Within a moment, the geopathic stress zone on White Street was gone and immediately the place felt different. The air was lighter for a start, the sounds of laughter travelled better.

The next weekend saw the annual Fire and Ice Show where sculptors armed with power-saws carve fascinating figures out of 300 pound blocks of ice. In previous years the ice works were displayed on High Street, now some were on White Street exactly where the geopathic stress zone had been. The Mill Race area was inundated with visitors and merchants reported a "great day." Whether it was the removal of a geopathic stress zone, I do not know. The energy and the people felt right.

It is always good strategy to check one's decree work so a day or so later Betty Lou and I cruised the old Mill Race area and found ourselves on East Monroe Street. It was a name we were going to remember.

In the soft afternoon sunlight of that winter's day, a large and stately tree stood alone on a newly dug and empty lot. But it was not the tree that caught our attention, but a colossal burr or gnarl, probably the size of a refrigerator, sticking out like a sore thumb midway up where the branches spread out from the trunk. As mentioned earlier the correct name is *tumor-type neoplasias.*

Without a doubt the tree deserved a photograph. To take the photograph I had to stand on freshly turned damp earth which in itself was puzzling, but what really caught my attention was a geopathic stress zone running through the tree. My feet and legs suddenly felt heavy, as if unseen hands were trying to pull me down. In that moment of time I was sharing the hurt, the struggle with which that poor tree had endured in pain for perhaps fifty years or more. (See PHOTOS #8 on page 111.)

"The tree is living in agony," I said back at the car. "It's living on a very strong geopathic stress zone."

Suddenly anxious, Betty Lou asked: "Can't you release the it? I don't like to think of a tree in pain."

"Something is telling me to wait," I said.

Little did I know that I was embarking on a major investigative dowsing case that would take us on a trek covering half a mile of the old Mill Race and downtown Mount Holly and even into the old residential area. It was 900 yards of pain, suffering and agony that had been going on since before the community was established by the Quakers in 1677. Unless it is a seasonal phenomenon — appearing every spring in the run-off period, a permanent geopathic stress zones will stay for centuries, perhaps eternity until there is a major shakeup in the land.

One of the great aspects of Google Earth is when an address is inserted, it not only comes with a view from space, but a click will bring you down to earth for a street photo.

So it came as a complete surprise: A picture of a house standing on the fresh earth patch in front of that lonely agonizing tree. (See PHOTOS #9 on page 111.)

THE HOUSE ON EAST MUNROE

Public real estate records revealed it to be 15 East Munroe Street, a single family colonial style cottage with upstairs and downstairs built in 1918 — one hundred years ago! Dowsing on Google Earth readily showed the geopathic stress zone to be substantial — 18 to 20 inches across, running over clay, broken rocks and minerals, some 900 feet down, and its route — a direct diagonal line ran right through the old tree and the home.

The sheer size and power of this toxic zone must have played sheer havoc for the innocent families who lived here.

Then the voices started. Not just a couple, but dozens, probably scores of voices. All clamoring to speak, all struggling to say their piece.

In metaphysical circles it's called Psychometry. Everything in the Universe possesses a memory. Place sensitive hands on a tree and it will tell you of years of drought, fires, prolonged winters. Place sensitive hands on the stanchions overlooking a port and you'll see and hear ships, warehouses and people of a century ago. Pick up a family heirloom and your mind will relay images of great-great-grandparents getting married. A fossilized bone at a Vancouver workshop showed dinosaurs in the Province of Alberta, Canada over 132 million years ago. Everything, even you the reader of this book, contain actions and memories that will be available for those who read energies for time immemorial. Metaphysicians and mystics call them the Akashic Records, and as I focused on the picture of the old house, the memories and voices flooded in.

There were angry voices mixed with children crying, shrill voices of women in pain and frustration. Men bellowing and grunting, totally frustrated, slamming doors. A woman grated: "Frank I told you not to rent this place. It's a hell hole. The devil lives under the boards."

Another voice: "Enid's gone. She poisoned herself."

A little girl in a light dress and bonnet said: "My aunt is taking me away. She says God has taken my mom and my dad to Heaven and my brother Tom has run away. When I tell my aunt that I hate God she beats me. I don't like anybody and I hate this place."

The desire to find out more about 15 East Monroe was now uppermost in my mind and the more we discovered displayed a horror story. Zillow, the online real estate marketing service showed the home had been repossessed in late December by the "lender" and the building demolished in January 2018 a few days before we found the site, hence the fresh earth around the tree.

Zillow also reports how long homes are on the market. 15 East Munro had been on the sales market for a mind-boggling 5,335 days — that's a staggering 14.6 years!

Real estate records over almost 30 years showed a list of individuals, banks, mortgage companies, Department of Veterans Affairs and two sheriffs who had owned the house. The top price was once $85,000. In 1998 it sold for a remarkable $10. In 2003 it was sold for $98,000 only to sell in October 2017 to the Bank of America for a lonely $100.

This powerful geopathic stress zone was not only playing havoc with residents lives, it must have been a virtual despair point for property owners, especially if they knew nothing of toxic Earth energies.

QUESTIONING THE OWNERS

Full of questions I returned to the site and started tracking the geopathic stress zone. It was now important to find out who else shared this monster under the ground.

Two Hondurans, a young man and woman stopped by in a van and said they had once been inside the house, but it felt bad so they didn't stay. But he did have information: The telephone number of the so called "lender" who repossessed the house was a mortgage contractors' company. Three staff members came on line, one was the local representative responsible for the Monroe house. None had any idea what a geopathic stress zone was and furthermore could not divulge the name of the previous owner because of privacy laws. Incredible!

"You are selling the lot for $67,000 and you claim its $42,000 below real value," I said. "If you got rid of the zone, it would make living there a pleasure instead of an agony." They took my name and number. They never called back.

The Google photo of the Monroe Street house showed a Philadelphia realtor's name and number. An Italian-American, he had no idea what I was talking about and anyway, he could not divulge the name of the owner because of privacy laws. So much for real estate.

Just when you feel the trail is going "dry", odd things start happening. Betty Lou had long wanted to visit a couple in Pemberton. Tom turned out to be a recently retired postal worker and yes! East Monroe was part of his route. "That house! Number fifteen!" he said excitedly. "A strange place. We never knew who lived there. People came and went frequently. Most never stayed a month."

Back at base and on Google Earth I started dowsing the entire geopathic stress zone. The signals were not only broad but strong indicating something more than just a water vein — it was a stream, sometimes three to five feet across — and really deadly. Something was telling us in no uncertain words — investigate! That was only the beginning.

The zone at the gnarled tree runs north to south. Scanning south with a pendulum showed the geopathic stress zone crossing East Monroe and cutting through a huge uninhabited building. An aging sign showed it has been the Community Press of Mount Holly. Doors with paint peeling off were locked. A faded sign yielded two phone numbers. "Not in service" said the phone company's robot. A Business License on the door showed the last issue — 2009!

The zone wandered off across Monroe Park which contains four baseball diamonds. It narrowly missed all and headed off under Rancocas Creek and a small forest beyond, which somebody said was the Township limit. Remember this geopathic steam was 900 feet under the surface.

THE NORTH SIDE OF THE ZONE

It was now time to track the geopathic stress zone on the north side of the great tree with the gnarled burr. A stone throw away is a large white building which turned out to be a set of long barns with two brick chimney stacks — a place reminiscent of the industrial age. Which indeed it is.

Google Earth showed the zone plowing straight through the old works building, then splitting up. One vein traveled east and once out of the industrial area, was tracked through the Pine Street residential area but strangely avoided any houses. It seems that people in history learned to avoid toxic areas.

The main north vein or stream came from the north and continued right underneath the old works complex.

The current owner, Audrey Winzinger, a lively and hearty woman said the original factory produced hydro-electric generators for waterways. "They became quite famous and were shipped to customers all over the world," she added.

The lady appeared slightly embarrassed when I started talking about geopathic stress zones but I did promise her a copy of this book.

It is truly amazing what the Investigative Dowser can find on the Internet. Research on Google Earth revealed copies of the 1874 Scientific American containing advertisements for Risdon's Improved Water Turbines. T.H. Risdon & Co., Mount Holly NJ.

By the mid to late 19th century, water turbines were widely used to drive sawmills, grist mills and textile mill equipment, often through a complex system of gears, shafts, and pulleys. They were local and the pride of many a home-town industrialist but they were gradually made extinct by the large electricity grid systems and hydro-electric dams.

Risdon's employed over fifty men at its peak and when it amalgamated in 1901 with another famous turbine manufacturer named Alcott the work force escalated to 85. One wonders how the workers could have endured hours each day, each week and each month without falling sick to the toxic energy radiating underneath the plant. By 1920 the Risdon-Alcott Turbine Company was history and the Mount Holly Foundry Company leased the huge building along with its geopathic stress zone.

We may never know how many employees suffered at Risdon's and Alcott's because when people are sick on the job because of geopathic stress, they often quit and move to other jobs or even leave town on a train — or hearse. The health of employees normally went unreported, at least in those days.

Apart from being used by furniture makers and dealers, the great foundry works has stood more or less idle for the last twenty years.

We spotted a hastily painted note on one of the doors of the old plant. "Mill Race Theatrical Company," and as the geopathic stress came out through their door we made a note to return and find out about the group. The rest of the geopathic stress zone was calling because the Dead Zone was far from over.

GEOPATHIC STRESS GOES DOWNTOWN

The path of toxic energy swept across the turbine factory parking lot onto Church Street, which contains sets of older houses, all well decorated and flourishing — except the end unit. The geopathic zone ran through that house — the back entrance and out through the front.

There was no one home at 34 Church Street. The inhabitants had long gone and an official notice was taped to the window. "Abandoned!" Public Records on the internet showed the house had recently been sold three times in one year.

Peering through a dusty window revealed a large room, bare and totally empty. The geopathic stress created the usual tingling and heaviness in my feet and legs. The dowsing rods followed the zone across the street narrowly missing a house opposite by perhaps two or three feet.

Crystal, a mother of two, and nearby resident came by with a great smile and a bundle of positive energy. "That house! Oh, people came and went. They never stayed long. Sometimes a month, sometimes a few days. Some claimed the floor is slanted."

This is a not an uncommon symptom of a geopathic stress. Dizziness and a feeling the floor is not level or the ground is not safe are strong hints that geopathic stress is at work from below. Betty Lou often mentions reaction when dowsing.

Crystal told me she was familiar with ley lines but not geopathic stress. After listening intently as I explained the toxic effect of subterranean water veins gone wrong, she asked: "What does it feel like?"

"Stand here," I suggested and pointed to the sidewalk. She did and a few seconds later uttered a cry: "That's incredible! My feet and legs are starting to feel so heavy."

"Well, imagine trying to sleep on that for eight hours every night and it starts to have an impact on your body — and in particular it starts to reduce the immune system."

"You should tell people!" she commanded and then promptly jumped into a car and sped off. Our research showed that Crystal was a young relative of one of the property owners who refused to talk when we visited his store.

The next visitor was a tall, fresh looking Mount Holly policeman who came strolling along the street and watched while I photographed the abandoned end unit. To my complete surprise he was totally fascinated with dowsing and asked some excellent questions such as "How do you dowse?" and "What does it feel like?"

Like Crystal before, I had the officer stand on the geopathic stress zone. "My boots immediately feel heavy," he said. "I would never have guessed it and I patrol this street quite a lot."

While I had had two citizens feel and understand geopathic stress zones, I wanted an official, someone with rank, to feel and understand the dangers of geopathic stress zones, before the toxic energy was neutralized. But first it was necessary to see what other damage the geopathic stress had done to Mount Holly.

Mill Street is a major thoroughfare through the town and to my surprise the subterranean water vein producing the zone was now split into three and that trio showed in no uncertain manner they were existent.

Empty store windows laced with cobwebs, fading realty signs, and an eerie feeling of hollowness enshrouded anyone who stopped to observe. The zones existed in three commercial properties and all three were unoccupied. One was a 9,000 square feet warehouse, boarded up and appearing dead was the largest building. Real estate records at the time of our visit stated the place was being "renovated".

Incidentally, a casual observer would not need a dowser to point out the warehouse had a geopathic stress zone running through it. A twisted tree stands on the sidewalk outside the warehouse and marks the spot.

Strangely, not all geopathic stress affects people the same way. Perhaps there are lapses or spaces in the clay that cause Earth energy to remain beneficial. This was apparent because one of the zones also passed through the office of Interface, which specializes in communications from wiring to fiber optics. A tall, bearded fellow named Stewart said his company had been operating the store for "many years and never felt anything." He did admit that he rarely stands still. Also on the sidewalk he did say: "My feet are tingling but maybe that's your suggestion."

Then he added: "Of course you know there is an underground stream running through this area?"

"That's exactly what I'm talking about," I said with a grin. "It is that exactly."

After passing through a large parking area, the three geopathic stress zones were discovered on Brainerd Street, an upscale but old residential area of Mount Holly. Here again, a similar story existed. The houses affected by geopathic stress zones were either "For Sale" or simply quiet and unoccupied. This is also the street where Mount Holly's first one-room school house was built in 1776 and is still preserved. A geopathic stress zones passes through it. It is a wonder that no one felt or reported the strange and dangerous energy manifesting in the historic building. Maybe they did and no one took any notice.

GETTING PERMISSION TO CLEAR

The Dead Zone runs some 900 yards through Mount Holly. Apart from Stewart whom we met, there was someone else we wanted to meet and that was the Artistic Director of the Mill Race Theatrical Group now occupying part of Risdon's old turbine factory.

Tom Greenfield is a Broadcast Media Professional. He graduated the Tyler School of Art, was Graphic Designer for the Office of the President of the United States, served 14 years as Art Director/Designer for ABC News in New York, served as 3D Animator for White Cherry Productions at the Tony Awards before changing directions, becoming Artistic Director for the fledgling Mill Race Theatrical Company in 2011 to oversee all aspects of their productions.

The Company has a core group of about twenty, said Greenfield, and they now call 30 Church Street, Mount Holly NJ their home. By blending a mix of practical modern effects and cutting edge projection technology, the Mill Race Theatrical Company creates feature-length productions that place you right in the middle of the experience.

When you first enter their domain, it looks nothing like an historic turbine factory, but more like a huge movie studio with theater style seats, lights, projectors, scenery, backdrops, plus a stage behind which are workshops for scene construction.

We talked for over 40 minutes during which time we discussed dowsing generally and our Mount Holly Project in particular. An open minded professional, he asked pointed and interesting questions on how dowsing via Google Earth works.

"I told you in my email that you have a geopathic stress zone running through the entire length of this old building," I said. "We are sitting about six or seven feet away from it." The line actually ran through several of the rows of theater seats and the stage.

"You mentioned you can clear this," he said. It was not a question.

"I need your permission."

"You have it. Clear it!" He smiled, then added: "Let me know when you do it."

It was a good encounter and I had achieved from someone in authority the permission to clear. Whatever else happens on this Project I had permission to clear.

But being an old reporter, I decided to go to the top. That weekend I penned an explanatory letter of the Mount Holly Dead Zone Project to Mr. Jason Jones, the Mayor. We also offered to meet the Council and any officials who might wish to be involved. On Monday, February 12th 2018 I delivered the letter in an enveloped marked "Confidential" to the Town Clerk.

Regardless of whether or not I would receive a response from the Mayor's Office, I decided to clear the entire Mount Holly Dead Zone on Thursday March 1st 2018.

"How to do it" was something that had crossed my mind many times. Decree clearing had shown that it would neutralize or clear a geopathic stress zone from one end of the subterranean stream to the other, in other words, from one joint or split in the vein or stream to the next joint or split.

The Mount Holly Project contained at least five sections, so each one would have to be affected by specific decrees, or would one decree cover the 900 yards. It was a challenge that I would have to face sooner or later.

So early in March 218 I decided to experiment. We had cleared a farm and its buildings in one stroke. In addition we had cleared several blocks of trees in a forest where we walk. A practice developed quite early was to bring up the situation on Google Earth and using the "Path" facility on the system, draw a line encompassing the geopathically affected area.

Using the Decree technique we addressed the geopathic stress zones running through the target area. The good news is that it worked. We tested it on Google Earth and the target area was now clear. More confirmation was needed. That day we drove into the old town and tested main points, including the tree with the bulging burr that had triggered the investigation. All clear!

This means that areas with multiple geopathic stress lines, even one half mile of toxic energy, can be transmuted and converted into all that is good and beautiful in one stroke. I thanked Holy Spirit.

After two months of research, visiting locations, taking photographs and writing, we walked away, wishing downtown Mount Holly a happy and prosperous future.

Well, it did not happen.

HELLO! A SECOND DEAD ZONE?

Dowsers bear no similarity to dedicated bloodhounds who continually search for problems. This one came straight on like a bullet. A second dead zone!

Betty Lou and I encountered this hidden geopathic stress problem quite innocently when we attended the St. Patrick's Day Parade in Mount Holly. These annual parades are substantial not only with highly decorated floats, trucks and cars. But also marching bands, musical groups on pickups and even a few clowns. Most come from Burlington County but some of the musical groups came from far away. It is a big annual event in old Mount Holly.

Several thousand people jammed High Street but at the T-road, they call it Fountain Square — one point was clear of spectators. For photography the place gave a splendid view of the parade coming towards us. I made the mistake of asking the Why? question. Why was this particular point deserted?

Scouting for answers we discovered some tell-tale empty stores and close to where we were standing — a twisted tree! If the reader does not know by now, twisted and contorted trees are signposts of geopathic stress.

Immediately behind the tree among the empty stores was a deserted restaurant. "Nelly's Express: Spanish Food. The Best in Town!" proclaimed the banner. Betty Lou said it had originally been a flower shop, then two different restaurants all within the space of five years. A "For Rent" sign graced the front door. (See PHOTOS #10 on page 112.)

Dowsing Google Earth showed a complete set of geopathic zones starting at a recently closed automotive repair shop on East Munro Street—a stone throw from the famous tree with the bulging burr. The zone headed through the old turbine factory through an empty house followed by the former restaurant, stores and offices and the twisted tree on Fountain Square.

Then it headed through the back of various stores including a couple of art galleries, across a large parking lot, before hitting the huge Burlington County Offices and Courts Complex. By now the geopathic stress zone was divided into several veins. One went through the Burlington County prison facility next to the courts. Another went through a house that had recently been rebuilt from the ground up. People do this in the hope of cleansing a "sick" building.

One very important point. This geopathic stress zone was only some 600 feet down, unlike the first set which ran over 900 feet below the surface. It is always good practice for the dowser to ask if there are any above or below the obvious ones.

Needless to say we were disappointed in the discovery. We had spent too long on the original project—two months—to start detailed work on another in the same town.

Who would give permission to clear? Visually scanning the Google Earth photo showed the newly discovered batch ran through the edge of the Mill Race Theatrical Company premises in the old turbine building. Tom Greenfield, the Artistic Director had given us permission to clear.

Less than a week after the St. Patrick's Day Parade the second project was fully dowsed and cleared using the Decree technique.

At the time of writing, it is now Fall in old Mount Holly and signs of revival are showing. Fresh "For Sale" signs are appearing and merchants in the Mill Race area are reporting changes.

Elaine who together with husband Mike own "Cheerful Dreams" a sort of far out metaphysical store that has everything told Betty Lou: "Since Robert cleared the zones we are getting more people coming into the area and our store. Things are looking much brighter now."

LOOKING FOR LEADS

Investigative dowsing can be as big or as small as the operator wishes it to be. Of course if one is in the least bit curious, it may well lead into something big with the likelihood of being controversial. But that's the way dowsing is right now, controversial and on the front lines you will find controversy difficult to avoid.

My rule is: head for the jugular! When I find it, Betty Lou takes over. If she meets an industrial mogul, a U.S. Senator, a highways and transport Commissioner, she plows straight in and starts talking dowsing and geopathic stress.

If you are looking for projects it is likely your search will be rewarded by recognizing a symbol of a twisted tree, an "Abandoned" sign on a house or factory, a report of a "sick" building, complaints from employees in a company of high rates of sickness, or a newspaper story of "bad energy" in a particular part of town.

Such occurrences as stores or houses frequently changing owners is a major sign that geopathic stress is a problem.

If you really wish to hit the big time use a search engine. Insert your town or area, and then write "Sick Buildings" and see what comes up. You may be amazed.

Sometimes they are just employees' complaints about ventilation, crammed quarters, illness, personnel problems, people quitting — all can be signs of geopathic stress. Get the address and dowse out the building on Google Earth.

Unfortunately it is quite easy to find toxic energy zones running through hospitals, clinics, factories, industrial complexes, government offices, shopping centers, yes, and even apartment blocks. Geopathic stress has no preferences or favorites.

Once a possible project has been found, set to work and dowse the entire route of the geopathic stress zones, even if they go on for hundreds of yards. Remember they are caused by streams running over clay, broken rock, fissures and other things. They can and do stop showing toxicity even though the water veins run on. A two mile subterranean stream may only be toxic for one part or several parts of its existence.

If the toxicity suddenly ends, dowse for where the vein goes and it may well "go toxic" again several hundred yards away. It all depends on what project you have decided to explore. Use the pin system on Google Earth to plot veins and streams and make notes. It is very easy to accumulate information and lose it because of a lack of notes, either on the laptop or on paper.

DEVELOP A GOOD HANDOUT

Early on in investigative dowsing we found the need for a brochure, a handout that explains in easy to comprehend two aspects: (1) the modern day faculty of dowsing, and (2) geopathic stress zones, how they occur, their impact on people and communities plus how dowsing can eliminate, neutralize the toxic effects and replace with beneficial energies.

The handout might include a description of beneficial energies such as leys and geospirals.

Then physically visit the location, confirm your dowsing record and see what's happening at the various buildings or sites. Make notes. Bent trunks and burrs on trees indicate a geopathic stress zone so check where its route goes.

If in an office, bank or clinic and staff appear irritated, unhelpful, check for geopathic stress. Always ask permission to clear from the owner, proprietor or someone in authority. Do not express your findings of "sick" buildings with employees because you may finish up in a law suit if there has been serious sickness among office workers. It is one of the reasons the remote dowser should always deal with the owner or the person in charge. Occasionally an employee will quietly request a clearing, such as Ellie and the health facility earlier in this book. Just do it but do not publicize it.

Points to remember:

When approaching a business speak on the subject only with the top manager.

Take photographs wherever you go. If ever you need to do a presentation, a workshop, write a book, information becomes invaluable.

Keep a journal on your activities, particularly if you get involved in a lengthy project. The Mount Holly Project took ten weeks before it was cleared.

A 'SICK" POLICE STATION

We almost forgot this story. Police District 5 in Cincinnati was big news in 2017. Newspapers and television news hounds followed the action over the months as reports claimed the building was "sick" with allegations of cancer among the 34 staff members.

Dan Hils, police union president, fought to get officers out of the old District 5 building on Ludlow Avenue. He said as many as 90 officers who worked in the building have contracted cancer and he is worried the building may be a health risk.

Curious, we dowsed the place on Google Earth and the scan showed two geopathic stress zones coming into the building, merging and then flowing out onto the highway. It was a Y-configuration.

On October 17th 2017 we emailed a report to the District 5 Police Commissioner with a dowsing report and offered to clear the toxic energy problem. We never received a response. (See PHOTOS #5 on page 109.)

By early 2018 the old building had been evacuated and the headquarters was relocated to another point in the District. Not once, in any published report was there an indication that geopathic stress may be the fault. If it had been cleared, it would have saved the city millions of dollars, let alone grief for those who were sick.

If you are into Investigative Dowsing always keep your eyes and ears open and your dowsing gear ready.

13

CASES ALONG THE WAY

In an age where the environment, foodstuffs and activities around are so often questionable, mothers are more prone to look after their children, especially in the younger years. Val who lives in Aston, Pennsylvania is one such mother.

Naturally sensitive, Val could feel strange energies around the home but did not quite understand them even when friends came over for dinner from ParaStudy, the local metaphysical group and mentioned strange energies. *"That was years ago and it did not have much significance for me then."*

"Now I am a mother of a five-year old who is otherwise healthy and he is a cancer survivor. This is why I need to look into geopathic stress," she said. *"My family tries to eat organic local food. My son was breast-fed until he was three. I make my own detergent, we don't own a TV and minimize screen time on the computer, otherwise he rarely goes to the doctor and no vaccines, Tylenol maybe twice."*

"Born at home, cloth diapered and carried in a sling, he tested negative for the expected genetic mutation, even though his extremely rare form of cancer is associated with mutation 70% of the time," she said. *"I could go*

on and on, but you get the picture. He had NO risk factors for cancer and had less toxins than most other American children."

Val then explained how this led her into electro magnetic sensitivity. *"We got the smart meter installed on our home next to the couch he wanted to sleep on about a year before his diagnosis."*

Val said her son had been sleeping on a couch. "I believe there may be a geopathic stress zone because I personally had experienced horrible sleep and intense nightmares when sleeping in one corner of his room. My boy slept on the couch because he never wanted to sleep in his room," she said.

"Even when he did, he would sleep on the floor instead of his bed," she said. Val added *"I've had increased or new mental health issues to deal with since I've moved into this home about a decade ago."*

"A friend on Facebook tagged me in a post with a documentary about geopathic stress and it makes so much sense," she said. ""Why didn't I think about that?"

"The Universe nudged me to contact you," Val told me. *"I learned about geopathic stress about two weeks ago. My five year old son is in remission from cancer and I was in Nemour's Hospital satellite office in Deptford waiting for my son's MRI to be done, when I picked up Natural Living magazine and leafing through, I spotted your face looking at me under the heading Dowsing, and I said Hey I know that guy."*

Val's note to us was dramatic and urgent. Her home in Aston PA came up and a scan showed a geopathic stress zone running west to east When it reached the center of the home it split into a Y-shaped configuration. Dowsing showed a subterranean water vein, some 600 feet below the home, running over clay, gravel and broken rock. A picture was emailed and within the hour the request came back "Please clear!" It was done at precisely 5.33 p.m. but it did not feel right. It left me wondering.

Next day Val emailed: "I was moving boxes down to the basement around the time you were doing the clearing. I did feel something, but it was like a resistance, then it disappeared. My son went to sleep in his room and came into our bedroom around 5:30 am, which is later than usual! Unfortunately I think the lines were crossing at the master bedroom, but perhaps things will improve from here. I'll write in a few weeks to let you know."

Val wrote back sooner. Apart from one day and night of peace, things were now upended. The doctor told her son that he was not suffering influenza but something close. In addition Val's crazy dreams were back and the cat was back on her bed — all bad signs.

Concerned, the case was reopened and a second scan of the property on Google Earth was performed. Starting the new search I remembered the pendulum had hesitated before finally indicating the geopathic stress zone at Val's place. Curious, I scanned the perimeter. Again a hesitation. Enlarging the picture and focusing on the area, the pendulum went into a full affirmation. Here indeed was a second geopathic stress zone and it crossed the arms of the Y-shaped configuration of the first zone Was it connected with the first which was reported as 600 feet below the surface? Absolutely not. This one was hiding 230 feet down.

Apologizing, I sent an updated picture with the second geopathic stress zone in blue.

Val came back: *"This blue line makes the most sense to me with respect to what I've felt over the years. Moving from left to right along the picture, it's entering the home right where our smart meter was installed, and where our couch is where P (the cat) started sleeping right before his cancer diagnosis. He slept there because he didn't want to sleep in his bed. His bed is situated in the far corner of his bedroom, where the blue line is exiting* the house. I cannot rearrange the furniture. It's such a small house, there wasn't another space where it really fitted."

Then Val added: "That corner of the house is where I've had my intense nightmares and limbic scary dreams."

The house was re-cleared and as a relaxation and healing force a Cosmic Principle — the plan of a pyramid with a diagonal cross — was placed in the yard. It was large enough to safely cover the home with Yin energy.

Two days later, Val told us: "The difference I feel in this house this morning is pretty amazing. I felt like there was a shift last night, though I know you did the clearing a couple of days ago. I have had some vivid dreams. My son and I were able to have a breakthrough kind of healing conversation last night. P (the cat) slept in his bed two nights in a row, with his head in the corner of the room that was so troublesome. My son had come home sick on Friday but this morning he woke up and came out of his room and said "I feel great!" He was further excited because it was not a school day."

Geopathic stress zones have a negative impact on wildlife. They disappeared until the toxic energy was neutralized. This happened with Val who wrote that she started seeing things differently: "This morning I watched the nor'easter clouds roll south, as the sun rose behind them. I saw a white goose in the flock that frequents the yard across the street. Then I was drawn by a sound to witness a squirrel munching on a nut. Last night I also exchanged glances with a deer. I know those last things sound irrelevant, but they feel significant to me and I wanted to share. We'll see how my son is feeling when he wakes up this morning, but so far, everything is much different!"

Three months later Val told me: "The energy in the house is flowing rather well in general. We do have a Mercury Retrograde going on, which *is highlighting emotional and relationship issues, but we're moving out of that. Things are relatively well here. I've been feeling better and better, but I do think that we all have some settling to do before we assimilate the full energetic effects. The image coming to mind now is when you make bone broth and you have to skim the scum, it's like that. Stuff is coming up, and we're able to process and get rid of it, rather than having it sink back into the depths."*

A LESSON LEARNED

Val's case mentioned above should have been sufficient for me to double check a property for a second geopathic stress zone hidden away, but it did not seem important at the time. It happened again, a few months later in April 2018 and it came as a shock.

Anita in West Caldwell, New Jersey wrote a long and detailed letter. She stated she had been with Diana Warren, a well known Princeton/Kingston energy healer who tested Anita's home for negative forces.

Anita wrote: "The pendulum went crazy when she asked if you specifically would be beneficial to clear my home. It said **Yes** emphatically."

Then Anita wrote this heart searing email: *"I have been trying to get well for years. My husband and I met in a bereavement support group. He lost his wife to breast cancer (we are living in the home he lived in with his previous wife).*

I've had autoimmune issues (psoriatic arthritis which is similar to rheumatoid arthritis) and became nonfunctional with that for literally years. I am not as bad now with that but not good.

I have fatigue and only have a little bit of energy to do something each day. Just washing my hair can be a big deal. I have had breast cancer, a second concussion, lymphedema post breast cancer surgery. I am cold most of the time. I keep getting sick and can't get back on my feet.

Pneumonia occurred last year secondary to the flu, left me more tired. Since December, I keep getting viruses or something, with 3 sets of illnesses with fevers. I barely recover and get something else. I've had swollen glands for 8 weeks now and the doctors haven't been able to help me. There are probably other things that I can't remember."

Anita's next sentence struck hard: *"You have already cleared my home of geopathic stresses in early November of 2017."*

My log showed the scan and clearing performed October 31ˢᵗ, 2017. I wondered why Anita had waited almost six months to get back to me. I always ask for feedback, good or bad — and this was bad.

Immediately I checked the address on Google Earth. Google keeps the scan on a user's access point until the user removes it. Anita's record of pins and yellow lines was still there. A pendulum confirmed the geopathic stress zone was completely neutralized. So what or where was the problem? Then Val's case in Aston, Pennsylvania came to mind — double geopathic stress zones!

Another scan of the West Caldwell property showed a second Y-shaped configuration. How on earth did I miss it in the original scan? They were both subterranean water veins flowing in the same northerly direction, in places parallel and shadowing one another. One was clay dominant, the other cracked rock dominant.

Were they connected? Not a bit. The original zone #1 was at a depth of about 700 feet while zone #2 was down even deeper at 1,100 feet. A second clearing took place.

From this I adopted a completely new scanning procedure. I had always scanned for other negative energies such as spirit entities, EMF, Radon, lightning strikes, but now I included the question: "Are there any other geopathic stress zones affecting this property that I may have missed?" This seems to fulfill the problem of missing a second.

The other part of this strategy is to make sure you get feedback from the property owner once when the building is cleared and then check a month or two later to see that all is well. Our records show we did not hear back from Anita since the initial clearing at the end of October until almost six months later.

This set me back to thinking about the wording of the decree. Until now my decrees had been zone specific. I now had to target "all geopathic stress zones known and unknown affecting this property now be transmuted and converted into that which is good and beautiful."

ANNA AND THE MYSTERIOUS HUM

Anna lives in a well designed single family home set among the luscious trees of Lawrenceville, NJ and when she bought the place it seemed ideal. But as the weeks and months rolled by Anna started to feel "distinct pressure" in the home and her sleeping habits were disturbed by a humming sound. It soon became so bad that Anna simply wanted to get out. It appeared no one had any solutions.

With Anna's address, a photo of a snug, 50-year old place half hidden by cedars came up on Google Earth. She confirmed the photo and when the home was dowsed, a Y-shaped configuration of a geopathic stress zone emerged. Dowsing showed it was 175 feet down and the water, flowing north over clay and broken rocks was permanent, in other words not seasonal.

When Anna received the map of the GSZ she responded: "May I call you Hero? You cannot know how relieved I am to hear this. This completely corroborates what I believe has been going on. Although my neighbor disagreed I had thought an underground spring ran through here. The house sits on a downward slope with surface water running from south to north to a natural stream beyond the houses across the street. Also the house trembles from time to time, as if some sort of seismic activity occurred , usually after midnight, though nothing is stated in the news anywhere about earthquakes occurring."

Then Anna revealed how the situation had impacted her life. "In the past two years, both my dog and I have developed health issues. I believe the hum has greatly contributed to my inability to sleep and dream, which impacts me greatly. My sleep patterns are disrupted, I wake stressed and tense and I cannot focus or concentrate for longer than four minutes at a time."

"I have to nap at least once a day in order to get enough sleep to function at all. In the past 6 months, I have developed heart issues, and other health problems. My dog, a sight hound, and highly sensitive, has developed nose and eye tumors. For me, ear plugs dull, but do not diminish, the vibrating sounds."

Anna asked that we should clear it immediately and this was done next morning at 7.49 and this information was emailed to her. The decree, typical of most of our others, asked that the negative, toxic energy of the geopathic stress zone be "transmuted and converted into that which is good and beneficial." The decree also added that all energies currently present and those to come would be "relaxing, healing, uplifting, inspiring and loving" for the next 100 years. This was a blessing that we developed in addition to the regular transmutation and basic clearing.

Anna replied: "I did feel a change, and a difference in the air and my breathing. But I still hear or feel the hum, although it is more intermittent than before. Will it gradually go away? Thank you so very much."

When a house is cleared by decree the change is instant, however if a person has been exposed to a geopathic stress zone for a prolonged period, the damage to the immune system and the body and mind may take longer to heal. But the body is resilient and normally good health returns.

"THE BIRDS HAVE COME BACK"

Wildlife does not like geopathic stress zones. One New Jersey lady told me that since her home had been cleared, the resident dove population had risen from two or three to about 20 and she added, some deer are visiting too.

Betty Lou and I often walk in the Rancocas Creek forest near Pemberton, New Jersey. The old railroad line has been developed into an easy walk, but one thing is notable most of the year — an almost complete absence of wildlife.

If the visitor takes a look at the trees, many are bent, contorted and generally malformed simply because of the presence of geopathic stress zones. But having said that we have both noticed that in south and central New Jersey that wherever forests or collections of trees exist there are many trees in agony, which means toxic Earth energy. Whenever we take a photo of a contorted tree, a victim of a geopathic stress zone, we always clear the zone and tell the tree we love it.

One tree that always catches our attention is on the walking path towards Pemberton. Both Betty Lou and I have noticed that the burr or wart on the tree is slowly but surely diminishing in size since we cleared it from a zone over a year before.

One wonders how many homes that have been built on previously forested areas contain geopathic stress zones contributing to sick health and possibly death. Visitors have told us there appears to be an abnormal number of clinics and hospitals in the state, a rather oblique sign of geopathic stress? (See PHOTOS #14 on page 114.)

An alert observer may observe we often clear trees when we find them without permission. There is an answer. When the dowser cannot find anyone responsible for providing that permission — ask Holy Spirit or whoever you think is in charge of life and the Universe. The answer will always be: "Go ahead! Clear!" You will be glad you did. It's a great feeling to release a tree from the terrible grip of a geopathic stress zone.

A STUNNING FINDING: A DYSFUNCTIONAL FAMILY

Permit us to paint a word picture of how the Silent Killer works and the real damage it is doing to people in all walks of life, their families and their wellbeing. Joan and John Homestead have just decided to buy a bigger house to accommodate their growing family. John is a vice president of a communications company and Joan is a stay-at-home Mom and fashion magazine writer. They have three children. Brody is 16, interested in Math and doing well in school, Connie at 14 is a natural artist and may well study fashion design. Bernadette at ten is a real tomboy at climbing trees, swimming and dreams of becoming a mountain climber.

When the realtor showed them the compact, single family home with four bedrooms, three bathrooms, a huge lounge and a similarly large sundeck flanking a cedar forest, it was a dream come true. They moved in as daffodils were blooming in the garden and an April shower sprinkled the place on their first day.

"That's a good sign," said Joan. "It is Nature performing a baptism."

Exactly two years later it was John who announced: "Sorry Joan, I think we've bought a sick house. This place is a hell hole."

The sickness was not apparent for some months. John noticed it first and complained of sleepless nights and a perpetual neck ache and weekly migraines.

Joan recalled the frequent complaints she made of "feeling tired". She became snappy with the children and called them "lazy!"

The pain in her legs which the doctor said were "imaginary" got worse, pain-killers did not seem to work and she missed three key deadlines on fashion articles.

Brody started getting bad marks in everything, became irritable, got dumped by his girlfriend, and refused to admit he was depressed. He frequently closed himself in his room and the depression increased.

Connie and Bernadette since they were very young liked to sleep together. They decided they hated the bedrooms upstairs and found a niche in the recreation room in the basement. That upset mother and father.

Their second Christmas in the house was a real flop. John came home and announced he had been "laid off," actually he was fired for insubordination and sleeping in the office restroom. It coincided with Joan being told to take "time off" from her freelance contract with the fashion magazine and the police calling to say Brody was found with a gun. "Your boy was in the park trying to kill himself. It was a miracle the gun jammed."

From this point on, the family started on a downhill run to becoming totally dysfunctional. Joan's parents loaned them money to pay bills, but it was not enough to handle the bills that kept coming in the mailbox. John sold his Mercedes and one day disappeared.

Joan got a job in a Department store as a sales clerk, Brody got a job at McDonald's. Their joint income was enough to feed the family but not enough to support the mortgage which had not been paid for months. One day in that third year two things happened within one hour: the doctor informed Joan she had cancer and when she opened her mail, there was a default letter from the bank with a notice of foreclosure.

They sold their furniture for what Joan termed "a pittance" and moved to a mobile home that her father had acquired on a plot of land he owned.

Little did they know and chances are they never will find out that their dream house was built on a double geopathic stress zone, toxic earth rays bent on reducing the family's immune system to the point it becomes dysfunctional and the bank forecloses.

The house stood empty for one year, its appearance was improved by some renovation and a new family moved in. The mother proclaimed "This is our dream home..."

"Ah, that could never happen to us," someone might say. "We don't believe in those sorts of things. The government wouldn't allow it, I mean, they have laws to protect us."

Really? Let us look at Foreclosure USA.

THE FORECLOSURE DILEMMA

If you can handle big figures imagine 676,535 foreclosures on U.S. properties in 2017. Let's reduce that a little. According to ATTOM Data Solutions, curator of the nation's largest multi-sourced property database in May 2018 alone there was a total of 71,949 U.S. properties with foreclosure filings, up 12 percent from the previous month but still down 12 percent from a year ago.

Seventy-two thousand homes! A little voice whispered in my ear: "Have you ever wondered how many of those homes are situated on geopathic stress zones?"

It had never occurred to me but now the investigative dowser was about to find out and the research results are stunning.

Insert "Foreclosed homes" in Google Search and a variety of sources will come up like Zillow, Auction, Realtytrac and Bankforelosuresale and you will receive long lists of foreclosed homes in almost every state.

Far from being an academic researcher, it is my old journalistic training that prods me to keep asking questions. On Google we typed "foreclosed homes in New Jersey." A long list surfaced so we took the first seven. The homes were in West Orange, Prospect Park, East Orange, Manchester, Millville, Passaic City and Toms River.

Each address was then brought up on Google Earth and each one was methodically dowsed and scanned twice. Each one suffered from one or more geopathic stress zones!

These small but alarming findings set off a series of checks on foreclosed homes in other states. We started with five properties drawn at random in Delaware: Seaford, Newark, Woodland Beach, Woodcrest and Dover. Each one possessed geopathic stress zones.

Next we scanned six foreclosed homes in California: San Jose, Clovis, Fresno, Modesto, Oakdale and a second one in Fresno. All were suffering with geopathic stress zones. It was the last one that drew our attention.

Situated on a quarter acre lot with five bedrooms and three bathrooms, covering 2,500 square feet, it was built in 1994 for single family use. The reserved price for auction was $744,386 plus 35 cents which was the debt at the time of foreclosure.

Listed for sale in November 2016 it was taken off the market in April 2018 after being viewed 873 times.

The problem? Well to get a mortgage to cover the $744,000, you would need a down payment of $148,000 and the ability to pay $3,559 a month. Which is not bad if you have an upscale job.

But to have a property viewed 873 times and no buyer? We dowsed the place and found three individual geopathic stress zones lacing their own criss-cross routes under the property. How the family who lost the home survived, only they and Heaven knows. But the clincher is this: to get inside the home those 873 viewers had to pass through two of the three geopathic stress zones that crossed either the driveway or the path to the front door.

From a dowsing point of view the home is a dead zone for anyone who buys it until the silent killers are removed. Tell some realtors this and they will probably throw up their arms and run away like cowards.

After California we checked properties in Arizona and Pennsylvania before turning to Washington DC.

Zillow will tell the enquiring visitor how long a property has been listed. Many foreclosed properties are usually picked up within a few days or a couple of weeks. Of the five properties scanned in the capitol city one had been sold three times in 13 years and had been empty for two years. It was a simple colonial style home built in 1941 with three bedrooms and one bathroom with a $219,000 price tag. Not bad for Washington DC.

A similar one with a $200K price tag had been on Zillow for 330 days.

But the one that really caught our investigative eye was the small palatial home with four bedrooms each with its own bathroom, a small ballroom downstairs and a price tag of $1.18 million. It had been listed for 643 days on Zillow. That is almost two years, so what was the problem?

It was a beautiful and well kept home but to get into it the viewer or prospective buyer had to walk through one of the four geopathic stress zones covering the entire home. The zones had an H-shaped configuration so that anybody who was in the least bit sensitive would feel the hostility of the place and walk away.

We concluded our off-the-cuff survey with six homes in Pennsylvania: Pocono Summit, Hatfield, Bethlehem, Dover, Harrisburg and North Wales. The last home, another four bedrooms affair at just over half a million dollars had a Y-shaped geopathic stress zone running through the place. But the back yard edged onto a major ley line running from Chester and the Delaware River through to Albany, New York and leys, as we have mentioned before, are positive, uplifting and beneficial. Without the silent killer below the home would be a great place to raise a family in safety.

In all we scanned 33 foreclosed homes and found geopathic stress zones in every one. If some professional surveyors working in collaboration with professional dowsers conducted a nationwide survey I sense the bottom line might be frightening.

Looking back one is reminded that the annual home foreclosures hit a record 2.9 million in 2010 and it is unlikely that anyone can speculate on negative Earth energies being a sole contributor to the dilemma. A portion, whether minor or major would have been fall-out from the American mortgage debacle of 2008 that undermined the financial stability of countries around the world.

A decade later and living in a reasonably stable economy, the investigative dowser can accept the fact that the vast majority of foreclosed home in the United States were and are being triggered by "sick" homes built over geopathic stress zones.

As we mentioned at the beginning of this chapter there were 676,535 foreclosures on U.S. properties in 2017 and that was a drop from previous years. Our small but significant studies show that it is possible that a large number of the folks who suffered the embarrassment of foreclosures were the victims of living over geopathic stress zones. A stark phenomenon that is known to reduce the human immune system and bring about prolonged sickness to the point the family becomes totally dysfunctional and loses its home.

SCIENCE AND THE TIP

Science recognizes the top of the problem — like the tip of the iceberg but fails to delve into the deep and consider Earth energy.

In January 2015 Science Daily ran a summary: "The mortgage strain of American home ownership can lead to poor health, but a new study finds that the inverse may also be true — changes in health can serve as a predictor to mortgage distress." How true!

The study, authored by two professors — Jason N. Houle (sociology) and Danya E. Keene (epidemiology-chronic diseases) showed that changes in health limitations and chronic conditions increased the risk of mortgage default and foreclosure. Middle aged adults whose chronic conditions worsened from age 40-50 have nearly twice the risk of mortgage default and 2.5 times the risk of foreclosure.

Chronic conditions in the study, included: cardiovascular disease and heart failure, lung disease, stroke, cancer, diabetes, hypertension, arthritis, asthma, joint pain and osteoporosis.

Professor Houle wrote: "It was surprising to us that so little research how becoming ill or disabled compromised household finances and increased the risk of default and foreclosure."

If only the researchers had looked under the beds.

If I were such a victim of geopathic stress I would start asking a lot of questions and demanding answers. But beware, nobody in authority is in a hurry to respond as we have discovered.

Letters were sent regarding questions on geopathic stress zones to various realtors, a town mayor and council, municipal administrators, a senior police officer in Cincinnati's District 5, the principal of a New Jersey school which was closed for a year, The Commissioner for the Department of Transportation in New Jersey and the Media Relations Officer of the National Transportation Safety Board in Washington, DC. At the time of closing this book for publication no one has responded.

The Silent Killer reigns supreme.

A CASE OF SPIRITS AND MORE

When Reddish first contacted us, her voice was cracked and barely understandable, so she emailed her problem what a letter it was. Reddish and her family live in a good and comfortable residential area of New Mexico not far from the Arroyo del Oso Golf Course. It has five bedrooms and 2.5 bathrooms and is a single level home in a place where the sun shines most days of the year.

Bluntly she told me that two of the previous homeowners died, one to suicide the other to alcoholism.

"I've been struggling with my health ever since I moved into this house 18 years ago," and she listed: Insomnia, procrastination, lethargy, auto immune disease and Hashimoto's (chronic lymphocytic thyroiditis), anxiety, fogginess, waking up tired after a full night's sleep, scattered energy and thinking, children fighting, depression and cancer. "Too many health conditions to name them all," she wrote.

But something else was bothering the family — entities! "I am always sensing someone in my bedroom at night looking or watching over me. After we spoke on the phone today my four year-old grandson saw an entity in the living room. My daughter sees them also, in the house and backyard."

Regarding EMF, Reddish wrote that the neighborhood is wireless and all cables are underground."

A Google Earth scan of the property showed the Reddish home had two permanent geopathic stress zones flowing through the house. The problem was compounded because each zone split into two parts, meaning the family had four geopathic stress zones passing negative energy up into the household. Dowsing showed that the first set of zones was at 840 feet below ground and the second set a mere 215 feet below. All were subterranean water veins flowing over broken rock and leaching minerals.

It was a tough scenario for any Mom and grandmother. It was made worse by a phenomenon known as Spirit Gate. If you are not aware there is a region in the Astral or Spirit World where negative inclined entities live their existence waiting for an opportunity to do something beneficial and migrate to higher levels. Sometimes they are inclined to play, yes, and even play havoc with families and people on Earth. You may have heard that positive people attract positive people and so it is in reverse. Negative entities are frequently drawn to negative energy situations here on Earth. It happens.

Geopathic stress zones frequently appeal to negative entities particularly when the victims are living and suffering from them. But their presence is not often appreciated. It's like a mugger trying to help a handicapped old lady across the road then making off with her purse.

Reddish would have been advised to tell the entity in her bedroom to "return from whence you came and go with love and light." But that takes presence of mind backed by good health and at that time she did not possess either one.

Since the clearing Reddish has got her life back on track. "I've gone through so much and welcome the positive changes."

When we did the scan mid-morning in early May 2018 there were no negative spirit entities on the premises and once it was cleared of geopathic stress the positive energy force would block any uninvited entities. The presence of negative spirits is an element dowsers must always search for when clearing a home or an office. This is in addition to negative Hartmann Grid points mentioned earlier.

A SPIRIT SLAMMED THE DOOR?

Most geopathic stress clearings are performed without a murmur. Some people hear books adjusting on a shelf, a photo falling, the air filled with a strange but likeable perfume, a breeze that seems to run through the house. It is simply just a change in energy from negative to positive.

There was one case that occurred with some sharp disturbance. When Candie's home in Florida was cleared, she reported: "My son had great difficulty as if a negative force left his body and at the same time, the back door sounded as if it had been slammed."

The geopathic stress zone in Candie's home not only created the normal insomnia problems, the condition caused her to gain weight. Oral gratification is one of the side issues that comes with geopathic stress zones. We sent her our CDs for weight loss and some months after clearing her home received the following: "This is a big change since you last saw me. The house is feeling much better. Thank you, Robert. Please feel free to use me to recommend your weight loss tapes. I did use them. They are great emotional support."

This goes back to our advice for Health professionals: A client has developed a problem concerning major changes in life such as overeating and putting on weight, ask "How long have you lived in your home?" Also: "How are you sleeping?" You may well find yourself opening the window to geopathic stress.

HOW A HOSPITAL FOUND US

While I encourage our fraternity to adopt investigative dowsing and always ask questions and find projects, sometimes the project will find us.

One day in early May 2018 Betty Lou wanted to visit an old and dear friend fighting for her life in Virtua's Voorhees Hospital in New Jersey.

Still a relatively new hospital, seven years old, it's the pride and joy of the non-profit Virtua Health System which is an extensive healthcare organization in southern New Jersey that operates a network of hospitals, surgery centers, physician practices, fitness centers, and more.

The Voorhees campus features a "digital hospital", a large outpatient facility and it facilitates 370 beds, each in a private room. Costing almost half a billion dollars to create, it was ten years in the planning.

According to the New Jersy Biz, a prominent business newsletter, the hospital "contains dozens of environmentally friendly elements and quotes five worth noting: 1. A glass curtain wall keeps heat in during the winter and out in the summer, maximizing heating and cooling efficiency. 2. Natural lighting is used throughout the hospital to decrease energy costs (not to mention giving patients a little Vitamin D), while outdoor lighting is designed to minimize light pollution. 3. Building materials were recycled and renewable whenever possible, and purchased from regional suppliers. 4. Some 40 acres of open space and wetlands were protected on the site; rooftop gardens further increase the green space. 5. Landscaping focused on water efficiency: native plants with rainwater irrigation should require little maintenance." That was in June 2011.

In June 2018 I dropped Betty Lou off at the main entrance to visit an old friend. In Parking Area A I discovered a place to park the car and settle down to a nice time of reading a book. The book was hardly opened when I felt myself experiencing a temporary loss of consciousness. A desire to sleep was brief but very noticeable. One would hardly notice it. Except I recalled it from earlier investigations reported in this book.

My rod went into search position. (One never leaves home without one.) A geopathic stress zone was inches away, its fringe toxicity affecting me. Outside the car I looked at the bushes on the border — all were alive and flourishing — except the one right in front of my car. That was dead.

The geopathic stress zone wound back towards the hospital. It sheared away from passing through the main entrance but several trees nearby were withered. In an areas where most pine trees flourish, one had lost most of its needles while dried cones still clung to the branches, almost grotesquely. (See PHOTOS #12 and 13 on page 113.)

Back at base, Google Earth showed the hospital and I quickly dowsed the geopathic stress zone that started it all. Within an hour my pointer and pendulum had tracked and recorded five other geopathic stress zones all trekking through the seven storied hospital.

Remember, a geopathic stress zone radiates upward. If one is in the basement, all other floors above are similarly affected. There are seven.

Betty Lou who is more diplomatic than her partner, called the hospital and asked to speak to someone who knew something about geopathic stress. The Plant Operations Director, Jim Twadell listened with the result I emailed our findings to him.

Surprisingly, a day or so later we received a reply. It has to be included in this book (1) because it's the only official response we have received during our study, and (2) it largely explains the challenges dowsers are facing, such as a lack of scientific evidence in the United States.

Robert, I appreciate your concern and thanks for your interest in my site and the wellness of those in and around it. I did do some research and discussed this phenomenon with my colleagues. There doesn't appear to be any robust research into what sort of mechanism might explain how a single phenomenon could account for such a wide range of medical and non-medical issues, and again nothing published in medical literature that I am finding. We're surrounded by technology that emits these sorts of fields. If they're not affecting us, then it doesn't make sense to claim that similar sorts of frequencies emanating from the ground will have any sort of effect. The bushes and trees that you saw dead or dying on our property is in my opinion more likely a result of road salt that often times kills trees as well as grass every year due to melting runoff and plowed snow during our winter snow and clearing of walks and roadways. This occurs yearly. I cannot explain your momentary loss of consciousness and though something that should be concerning to you . I am not in agreement that this occurred because of the phenomenon that you are describing . I again appreciate and respect your opinion but at this time we do not wish to pursue your offer of remedying this for us and will NOT be offering you permission to perform the service that you are offering . Thank you and wish you well. Jim Twaddell, Plant Operations Director, Virtua Voorhees Hospital.

TO CLEAR OR NOT TO CLEAR

The above case brings up the very delicate debate: "Should a dowser with information clear and heal a building — home, business or even a hospital — without the owner's or a representative's consent?"

Some voices might say "Yes, do it anyway." So what happens if the dowser clears the building and it becomes public and the very next day some disaster occurs in the building. Who will be the recipient of pointed fingers — and worse, legal action? The dowser.

The problem starts even earlier. Once a dowser acquires information that a geopathic stress zone is affecting any particular structure that could affect human health values, is the dowser honor bound to inform those responsible for the building and the safety of the residents or employees?

In the course of researching and writing this book scores of business buildings have been scanned through dowsing and found to contain geopathic stress zones. Management has been duly informed either through letter or email and no responses were forthcoming. The Virtua Hospital and the Mill Race Theatrical Group are the only exceptions.

Facing the question head on, possession of knowledge of geopathic stress zones affecting any form of habitation is simply a liability. All the people whose homes have been identified as affected by geopathic stress and which have subsequently been cleared, neutralized, healed in whatever way you wish to describe, should that information be passed on to incoming families?

Or should such knowledge be left, forgotten, as would events such as storm damage, infestation by ants, a car struck the cornerstone, etc?

And what about geopathic stress zones affecting intersections, streets and highways? If the authorities responsible for that property know of such threats to drivers, at what point do they become liable?

Which gets back to the original question: If a dowser intentionally or unintentionally acquires information on geopathic stress possibly affecting human habitation and wellbeing, should he or she be responsible for disseminating that knowledge to the appropriate people?

And furthermore, should a dowser with healing gifts or abilities be available to safely neutralize or heal the geopathic stress zone in question? It should be recognized that technology exists to effectively combat geopathic stress which can always be an option.

The failure of various people and organizations to even admit that geopathic stress zones exist and are undermining the health of the country reminds me of an anecdote Thaddeus Golas used in "The Lazy Man's Guide to Enlightenment." He focused on automobiles.

"If you refuse to admit that automobiles exist, you are going to get hit by cars not because you are sinful or neurotic but just because you are not looking at automobiles. You won't see them coming."

For automobiles read the geopathic stress crisis.

THE ANGELINA STORY

Angelina was a little lady behind cute circular spectacles, stressed and uptight as a violin string. For a Leo, born in early August her usual energy was running low. She said she had seen my name in a New Age magazine and had come for a psychic reading. I told her I rarely do readings while I'm involved in research and writing a book, but she persisted.

"I kept looking at your advertisement until something told me to come," she said, readying her recording device.

Her energy showed she had lost something that was driving her crazy. It was not a family member, a lover, a friend, it was as if her whole being was being drained both mentally and physically. She nodded to everything I said.

"I'm stopping the reading," I said.

"Why?"

"It's your home. Its not right," I suggested and that opened a floodgate. So I switched to my dowsing hat.

"The place smells. Wherever I go in the apartment there is always a smell. I cannot sleep. I keep waking up. There's no breeze. I have a fan on but the air is stagnant," she said almost on the verge of tears. "My friend Coral says the same thing. She has the apartment across the hall."

They lived on one of the higher floors of an apartment complex in Pennsauken, New Jersey. Angelina, aged 62 had moved into the two-bedroomed apartment seven months before. This was about time for a geopathic stress zone to make itself felt.

"I have just started to have trouble in my body," she said. "My knees hurt when I wake up and for a few days there I felt I had a hernia. I've never had trouble before."

A sprightly 62 years, Angelina is an African American. Since attaining a Business Major she has worked in various occupations, physical therapy, day care, jewelry and in the legal section at a county office complex. Her small body contains the energy of a go-getter.

Somehow wherever she lived she always encountered problems. Unknowingly, she had entered the geopathic stress zone trap, that is unbeknown to herself, she aligned herself with the strange toxic energies manifested in homes. Some people are like that. It can happen that when a sick person's bed is moved off a geopathic stress zone they often insist on being moved back, regardless of care-givers' protests or explanation. Angelina was like that. Even when she bought a house.

"I really liked the home when I moved in," she said, "but as the months passed my health deteriorated, I lost my job, my savings and when they talked about foreclosure, I just gave the place back."

On Google Earth her Pennsauken high-rise came on the screen. Angelina pointed to the floor where she and Coral had the end apartments.

Using a pendulum I scanned the building. Sure enough, a geopathic stress zone ran straight through both apartments. Angelina was stunned and hurt.

"The geopathic stress zone is about 750 feet below the building. A subterranean water vein is flowing over clay and broken rocks," I said. "It's sending toxic rays up through every apartment below you, through yours and those above."

Biting her lips, she was trying to comprehend.

It was then I decided to clear her home. I normally perform decrees while alone in my office, but now was different.

Angelina watched in amazement as the clearance was performed. "In the name of the Holy Spirit, I decree….. and furthermore this home will be filled with positive Earth energy that is beneficial, uplifting, wholesome and loving, and this decree will be in effect for the next one hundred years."

"What about the other apartments underneath and above?"

"You cannot clear one floor of an apartment block," I explained. "They have all been cleared."

"A lot of people are going to sleep better tonight," she said with a smile.

Then Angelina surprised me with another story.

Her sister Marion and husband Josh owned a nice row home, built in 1922 in Whitman Park an area of Camden, New Jersey. "It was a good home for a growing family," said Angelina happily but then she paused and her face saddened. "The trouble started first when their young daughter died, then a while later Josh died of prostate cancer. Over time Marion had many problems in dealing with her growing son. He was always gripped in bad moods with depression and admitted that he was gay. He finally left home."

"So Marion was left all alone," I added.

"Marion was the last to pass in that house," she said. "Pancreatic cancer. It was very fast."

While she sat there I brought up the Camden row house on Google Earth and scanned the place. A geopathic stress zone ran straight through the home and somehow they had lived and suffered with it to the point of death for 19 years.

"If only someone had told us," Angelina said with a sigh.

The Silent Killer had won again.

The good news is that with Angie's permission the home was cleared to a safe condition for all eternity.

LIVING WITH A DOUBLE KILLER

Most of the people encountered during our research and dowsing practice have either had a bad experience with geopathic stress at home or the office, so it is unusual to hear of a young man who has tolerated both and survived.

Rob said he heard about us because his wife Alice attended one of our psychic workshops in Mount Holly. Rob wrote: "Hearing about this made me realize that maybe our home and my workplaces are sick." The couple own a two family home and live on the second floor. It is situated in Central New Jersey across the Hudson from Manhattan and New York and they have been living there seven years.

Rob's letter on geopathic stress is classic regarding how the negative force undermines one's health to the point a person becomes dysfunctional. So we quote it here.

"The first year here was great but after that we started having problems with our next door neighbors who are extremely mean people. We also started noticing that we weren't being intimate with one another. I started developing an acute loss of energy, feeling very tired all the time, and having feelings of anxiety and depression. All these lead into seemingly constant panic attacks.

"Last year, my health deteriorated and I ended up at the Mental Health Hospital for five days. In this past year I've lost thirty pounds because I just cannot eat. My anxiety gets in the way! I have been so sick. I have been having terrible night sweats and some mornings I wake very nauseous and vomiting. I have been taking anxiety and depression medication and I have been visiting a psychiatrist, but none of this is really helping.

"I am also a very spiritual person, I do Reiki and Shamanism, but spirituality is not helping either. It alleviates the situation when I meditate, but soon all the bad feelings and emotions come back.

"My work is also very stressful. I work for a very demanding pharmaceutical company and they drive me crazy. Most days I don't want to go to work, the energy there is very heavy. They used to do experiments with animals and I know many of the creatures died there. No wonder if there are entities of some sort!

"I pray you can help me. I can't take feeling like this any longer! I cry all the time, and sometimes I feel like disappearing."

Rob provided the addresses of both the home and the offices where he is employed. When they were dowsed, it was found that a geopathic stress zone virtually split the home in two. A permanent subterranean water vein about 12 inches wide and 260 feet below the surface running over clay sent a shaft of toxic energy up through the home. That on its own would have generated many of Rob's problems.

Rob's workplace was then dowsed to find a geopathic stress zone created by water running over broken rock and leaching some 1,200 feet below the surface. It cut a swathe across the building before creating an upside down Y-shaped zone right through Rob's office.

Surprised that the place had not been described as a "sick" building, we checked with the Glass Door. Remember we are Investigative dowsers! The Glassdoor (or glassdoor.com) is a website where employees and former employees anonymously review companies and their management. Rob's company showed over 2,500 complaints ranging from prolonged work hours, lack of compassion in management, general irritability among staff, being disliked, lack of executive leadership, bad air conditioning, dirty floors — everything that official America uses to describe a "sick" building. No one mentions anything resembling geopathic stress or toxic earth energy. Yet these were all the symptoms.

When shown the Google Earth scans with the geopathic stress zones laid out, Rob said" Everything makes sense. Please clear both places." Shortly after 5.00 p.m. on September 13th 2018, eight hours after receiving the cry for help, and using Job's Decree technique the home and Rob's workplace were cleaned and replaced with beneficial, uplifting, healing and inspiring energies.

While the home and workplace energies were changed in an instant, it will take days, perhaps some weeks before Rob's health is back to normal, but at least he and Alice are on the road to a healthy and lasting union.

"Thank you for what you do," said Rob in a note.

THEY LOOKED FOR A DREAM HOUSE

They were old spirits. Both had suffered in different ways. Both had never married until they were in their forties. Both wanted a dream house in the hope that their trials were over.

Dave was born in the early 1950s when polio was still rampant and a handful of years before Dr. Jonas Salk came up with a vaccine that would change the crippling effect of the disease. Polio left Dave with life-long foot and leg problems. He pulled out of studying to be a Political Science Major and found work and settled into computer training.

Jessie had a problem with alcohol in her early adult life but had been "dry" for a dozen years when she met Dave at a spiritualist oriented church in Pennsylvania. Even before they met, Jessie had a small problem with her esophagus.

It was love at first sight, said Dave. "I asked Jessie to find a home," and she did. "A nice comfortable home in the country. It was relaxing and we looked forward to the rest of our lives together." They were both in their early forties.

Unknown to either that "relaxing" home had a geopathic stress zone running from one end to the other. The problem with Jessie's esophagus increased and she underwent surgery. "After surgery she was moved from the ICU too soon — a bureaucratic mistake," says Dave. "Not one year in, my beloved wife Jessie died at the age of 43."

The shock of Jessie's death plus the presence of the Silent Killer below played havoc with Dave's life. He was swept into a yin-yang depression that roller-coasted over the years. He lost his work, then his car and spent "every day for several years in bed, being taken food shopping once every one or two weeks." All the time he was living with the effects of polio and geopathic stress..

Occasionally he would find solace sitting outside the back of the house with a backdrop of forest-covered hills and a meadow at the side. "It was Jessie's favorite space too," he said. It was the south side.

Dave found me through a local dowsing workshop and asked to check his place. Back at base, I scanned his home on Google Earth and found a geopathic stress zone running along just inside the north side of the home and the main entrance.

Eighteen years after Jessie's passing, Dave gave us permission to clear. It was done remotely on July 12th 2018 at 10.40 in the morning.

After a few days Dave said "I feel optimistic. I am more active than I have been for a long time. I'm sleeping better too."

Then he said: "I'm spending time at the back, could you check the place for those geospirals you mentioned in the workshop?"

It was a hunch that paid off.

When we scanned the meadow next door we found a nest of six geospirals all radiating beneficial yin energies — a minor vortex. The lead geospiral — the Alpha — was radiating 35 rings out of a possible 49, making it a very good size, and the Geospiral #5 with 21 rings was centered just over the fence from Dave and Jessie's home. The geospiral energy was covering the home and could account as to why the geopathic stress zone had not sent Dave to his grave. The positive energies of the geospirals had seemingly mitigated to some extent the powers of the geopathic stress.

We emailed Dave the good news on geospirals. Back came a very short but heartwarming response: "Thank you oh so much, Robert!"

TESTIMONIALS

During the fifteen months we were researching and writing this book we had the opportunity of scanning and clearing geopathic stress from 158 homes and properties from many parts of the world. These were some of the testimonials that came.

"Robert, you are remarkable and a blessing. I'm still in bed this morning and woke up to take a full breathe of air that filled my lungs. It felt clear. My lungs felt full, clean and I KNEW you did something. My nostrils are not stuffy or dry. I can't wait to get up out of bed and not struggle to breathe heavily and pant up and down the stairs while struggling for air. THANK YOU already!!!!!" — L.B. Denville, NJ.

"Dear Robert, since you cleared my land, it is extraordinary how many birds nests I see there now. Before, I saw ONE. I have even bought binoculars to start bird watching!! Also, my neighbor, who I had a bad relationship with, came over for a misdirected package, and was NICE to me. I hope that this continues, as it warmed my heart. I will continue to keep you posted, as you requested." —C.S. Dexter NY.

"Thank you so much for the work you did on my house. It does feel calmer and easier to be in. I also have noticed my animals feel more relaxed." —S.M. Wallingford, PA.

"Thank you so much for the clearing. The house feels lighter and we all slept last night which is very unusual! I am feeling very cheery this morning so that's brilliant." — Y.F. Kirkwall, Orkney, Scotland.

"I was happy to hear that there is no geopathic stress zone affecting my home. Thank you for the information on crystals and for the Cosmic Principle you placed in my backyard. Here is a donation for the help you have given me. Blessings." — J.A. Elmira, NY.

"Dear Robert: Walter is absolutely thrilled by his home clearing. He now is able to get from his bed in the morning with less pain and every day he is feeling so much better to the point he is able to walk without a cane." —M.B. Elmira NY

"I wanted to tell you how much our house has changed these last few days. There was an immediate change but as time goes on the change is incredible. My cats are so much calmer. I think they are very sensitive to energy and react by running around and generally acting out. I know my foster kitten has become another animal. He is calm and has stopped jumping on the counter and my husband has even been waiting to clean up his clutter." —D.F. Doylestown PA

"Thank you for the clearing. I have always had concerns with my backyard because of the walnut trees we have. I haven't been able to grow a garden (vegetable) there." —S.K. Elmira NY.

"I initially and briefly noticed a sweet odor (pleasant) that I hadn't noticed before. I was curious about that. The ongoing impact is that I'm not waking with a headache every day! I may also have more energy, but I don't want to speak too soon on that! Again, thank you very much." —C.S. Corning, NY

"Robert-I DID feel a difference last night when I came home and I actually woke up this morning without any body aches or pains and I now feel more peaceful than I have in years. Thank you from the bottom of my heart. Blessings to you for this important work." —D.W. Lawrenceville, NJ

Robert, I wanted to let you know that things are so much better in my home. I will tell you how it started. I noticed as I was moving from one

room to another that my body was very tense. Picture how your body would feel if you were out shopping during the holiday season. Tense and ready to fight through the crowd of people. Well as I felt this tenseness I literally stopped in my tracks. All of a sudden at that moment I realized there was nothing to fight through. It was like my body realized whatever was once in my home that made me feel like that was gone. The house was free flowing. I no longer had to "fight" my way through my own home. It was a very, very weird realization. What was happening? What had we been exposed to all of these years living here? My mind was literally trying to wrap around what I was feeling. It felt so freeing. We also realized how relaxed we are. We feel at ease. Something we haven't felt in about a decade. I don't think we really realized how tense we were until that feeling was gone. It's very strange but great to feel like this! I never want this feeling to end. My body just feels so much better and my family is happier. Thank you so much! —C.H. Mount Royal, NJ

.I am sleeping better and having interesting dreams... I wish I could remember them more clearly!! But since the clearing my dog who passed two years ago has started to visit me in dreams. First time since his passing! Guess he's happy the stress zone has been cleared!! —M.M. Elmira, NY

I'm noticing subtle energy changes in different areas of the house... I take note that something feels different and then ask, "Is this my imagination or am I actually feeling differences?" I can almost breathe easier—and yes it is lighter. My husband made it until 5 am today instead of getting up at his usual 3 a.m. I still went to bed late but my daughter and her boy friend arrived late and wanted to visit so that enters into the equation. I didn't even tell my husband that the clearing took place. I will simply document to see if there are changes. Am very relieved and grateful that you were able to do this. — M.G. Corning, NY

Dear Robert, Thank you so much for clearing our house and property and so promptly. We did hear unusual noises around and inside the house throughout the day yesterday: My husband commented several times that the wind was whistling outside with a sound we haven't heard here in the past — and he doesn't know anything about this! I heard new metallic sounds in the kitchen, and different creaking sounds above our bedroom. All very intriguing! With love and smiles. — L.H. Princeton/Kingston NJ

Dear Robert: Thank you for the clearing of my house and the neighbors'. Many subtle and interesting things have happened. One thing is I have been able to put in place some consistent things that have always been elusive to me. I was always doing external things and just getting by with household chores. I am feeling more and more that I enjoy being a homebody and want to do things around my home. I wonder if the Hartmann Grid point was holding me out of my home or at least not wanting me to be here that much. I plan to help others as well too. May blessings to you. — M.P. Rochester, NY.

TRAINING HEALERS EARLY

Children, whether their parents know it or not, make good sensitives, in other words their tuition is blooming through the ages of five and eleven. It's at this point that the youngsters become gripped and enmeshed in the adult philosophies and limitations of grown-ups around them and also their older peers in the education system.

Children no longer have the ability to see and even talk with spirits because that part of the brain enters its prison, or to put it another way, the cage doors are shut. As you will have discovered in reading this book, it affects the male of the species more than females.

It would be advantageous for the American school system to adopt higher awareness training for students at an early age, say seven or eight. Teach them how to meditate, how to continue to see auric colors around people, and show them that the human body is a priceless gift of the Creator, the Cosmic Forces of whatever Higher Power they feel inclined to believe in. Teach them the values of self-love and as Paul of Tarsus wrote: "Make love your aim and earnestly desire the spiritual gifts."

Whether Dowsing itself constitutes a spiritual gift, I don't think so. It is an intuitive function of the human body that allows the Higher Consciousness to answer questions, provide guidance when required.

Now, when the Dowser Heals, that is a spiritual gift. When I remotely clear a home or an office or a farm stable by Job's Decree that is healing and it is a spiritual gift. It is focused intense prayer aimed at a particular target. As we explained in that section, I have no idea when the cleaning of negative energy such as geopathic stress takes place, but it does and it happens in a split second.

Several people who have attended my workshop on this subject have gone out and done the same thing. Therefore it is an acquired gift.

Students learning to use these gifts could embrace healing trees whose lives are impacted by geopathic stress. Bent and contorted trees often with ugly growths of burrs are symbols of this tragedy. They provide an excellent opportunity for students to learn how to find such trees, dowse the geopathic stress zones and conduct a neutralization of the toxicity. It would give young people a better appreciation of trees and prepare them for handling bigger projects as they mature to adulthood.

As the reader will have recognized, there is a national if not an international problem caused by toxic Earth energy. Geopathic stress through undermining the human immune system is in dire need for an army of young and well trained dowsers, working with scientists as they do in India, to tackle the massive problem of America's "sick" homes.

Such a force of young people would change the face of the country. Because from my experiences related in this book, there must be millions of people suffering needless agony in pain, sickness and the loss of loved ones.

Remember these words: If, because of your limitations and beliefs you are opposed to dowsing and healing geopathic stress, you are part of the problem and the Silent Killer Below reigns supreme.

I wanted to write THE END here but thought there are many who might like a glimpse of some positive energies, namely Leys and Geospirals.

14

SPECIAL SECTION: BENEFICIAL ENERGIES TO KNOW

THE PHENOMENON OF GEOSPIRALS

If you have a geospiral turning out beneficial Yin energy in your yard consider yourself blessed. Mostly, they are found in parks, churches, cathedrals, community centers, in quiet forests, monasteries, Native Indian spiritual centers such as pueblos and kivas.

They are great for meditation, relaxation, healing and if you like, excellent for chatting with ancestors, loved ones and others in Heaven, the Spirit World or whatever you call the Great Beyond.

Here are some notes that may help the reader understand.

GEOSPIRAL FORMATION: It takes two things to form a geospiral. One is pure water from deep underground and the other is a large rock shaped like an inverted saucer. This is what dowsers call a "blind spring" or a "water dome." When the water is under pressure from below, it creates a force under the captive rock which seeks a way out. Energy transverses through the rock and out from the rims. This energy spins into various circles or spirals. Once a nest of geospirals is found, a seeker will often find small springs feeding creeks.

A TREASURED SYMBOL: The Native Indians have a symbol for the Cosmos: It is a spiral that starts from the center and the lines rotate outwards, much like a hurricane if pictured from above. A geospiral has a similar radiating image. It should be pointed out that the geospiral while radiating outwards also creates a dome usually 20 to 30 feet above its center. When several are gathered together they radiate more energy beyond the rings. We call this an Area of Influence.

DOWSING FOR A GEOSPIRAL: Set a rod in the search position and ask if there are any geospirals within a quarter of a mile of where you are standing. If the rod twists round and stops it is indicating a spiral. Start walking with the single rod in the search position. When you cross the center point of the geospiral the rod will immediately swing round and point the way you have come. Walk back until the rod swings back and forth and you know you have a geospiral's center.

The next step is to measure the rings. Standing on the center location of the geospiral and holding both L-rods in the parallel search position walk away from the center. The rods will cross every time you walk over a ring and then immediately swing back into the search position. Count the number of times it shows you a ring and you have the power of the geospiral.

COUNTING THE RINGS: Strangely a geospiral will consist of seven and multiples of seven rings or bands. In other words — 7, 14, 21, 28, 35, 42 and 49. Seven ring geospirals are the norm and if you find a forty-niner immediately check for other geospirals in the area. In fact, the moment one finds one geospiral, immediately check for others in the area.

LOOKING FOR THE ALPHA: Your chances of finding the Alpha or Major geospiral in a nest is quite likely. They normally have a lot of rings and overshadow most of the others. In fact when you are dowsing for geospirals always ask the search rod to "look for the Alpha geospiral." Once discovered and measured, the dowser can ask for Number Two, Number Three and so on. Do not be surprised if you find smaller geospirals operating within the rings of the Alpha. It is best to use landscape markers when plotting a nest of geospirals.

MEASURING THE AREA OF INFLUENCE: Now if you do find a seven or nine vortex stand at the most powerful of the geospirals and say: "I wish to measure the area of influence of these geospirals." Please cross the rods when I reach the edge of the area. Start walking. You may be amazed. It may be half a mile or more. The Blue Lake vortex at Taos radiates for several miles but does change with the weather and moon. One aspect that is difficult to measure or see is that most geospirals when working together not only produce a combined area of influence horizontally but a globe of energy above. Some dowsers speculate it is a reflection of the rock underneath.

BEWARE! THEY MOVE! Geospirals have irregularities: You may mark the center of one on Friday and bring friends to see it on Sunday to find it has moved several feet. So you-re-stake it and return another day only to discover it is back at the original position.

GEOSPIRALS AND WATER: Expert dowsers like the late Dennis Wheatley in the United Kingdom suggested that most geospirals are indicative of blind springs, underground domes of pressurized water. We ascertained that most of the geospirals found in New Mexico, New

Jersey and Upstate New York are over blind springs and very close to running streams.

TREES ON GEOSPIRALS: A point discovered. When a tree grows over a geospiral the tree sprouts several strong and healthy trunks all blossoming from one point. They can be found in various forests that line footpaths. There's no malformation as you will find with geopathic stress zones, these trees are healthy growing on beneficial Yin energy. (See PHOTOS #16 on page 115.)

WHERE CAN ONE FIND GEOSPIRALS? The answer is anywhere. The easiest ones to find in the U.S. are those places once inhabited by Native Indians. They knew where the energy centers were and the health benefits that came from them. They also knew that if one gathered round a major geospiral one could talk with the spirits of ancestors.

Today we find many churches have been built with a geospiral within its walls. At the Cathedral in Santa Fe in the Chapel of the Blessed Sacrament there is a geospiral just in front of the altar radiating healing energy for the congregation. At the Chapel of the Blessed Sacrament that adjoins the Sacred Heart Church there is a geospiral in front of the altar there.

The building of the Catholic Church of the Immaculate Conception in Brownville near Watertown in northern New York State started as the Universalist Church in 1854 which became defunct and was bought by the Catholics in 1900. Again there is a geospiral just in front of the altar.

If you wish to find geospirals, look around your local church. Colleges and universities are popular sites for this phenomenon.

THE MOVING CAR SEARCH METHOD: One method of finding geospirals is to sit as a passenger in a moderately moving car (20-30 mph) and holding one L-rod, ask to show any geospirals within a quarter of a mile range. As you travel along you will find the rod starting to pick up geospiral activity in the distance and then swing round as you pass. Make a note of any cross roads and return to the area on foot and using one L-rod walk in the direction indicated.

LIVING ON OR NEAR A GEOSPIRAL: One interesting situation came to light a few years back. In Marlton NJ there was a family with a geospiral in their front yard. We discovered it while searching for a geopathic zone that the family believed was affecting the home. There was indeed a geopathic zone cutting across one part of the house close to where a baby slept. We cleared that.

Here's a suggestion if you are searching for geopathic stress zones always ask if there are any geospirals or an area of influence affecting the property.

The mother at the Marlton house told us: "We have all the children's toys located at the back of the house but they always bring them to the front yard and play with them there. Not once in a while, but always!"

The spot? Exactly on the center of the geospiral.

THE SACKETS HARBOR PHENOMENON: This popular tourist community and historical site should be dowsed in its entirety. The Battleground Park which dates back to the War of 1812 manifests several geospirals, particularly in the area of the Gazebo Picnic facility. There are at least nine geospirals clustered there and several others scattered along the Battlefield. Dowsers should check for an old well originally used by the military. We found another geospiral near the old Water Tower at Madison Barracks. Interesting point: If the dowser is quiet he or she may still hear Native Indian voices echoing through the mists of time. Sackets Harbor was home to a strong Indian community before 1800.

THE SPIRITUAL SIDE: Geospirals are not just something to dowse or measure statistically, they do have a spiritual side. A good sized geospiral is a wonderful opportunity for those inclined to conduct a meditation circle within the energy rings.

Remember Native Indians built their spiritual centers round geospirals and then talked with the spirits of the ancestors. If you have a spirit communicator (medium) attending the circle that will enhance spirit activities. If meditating, say prayers to raise your vibrations and protection from negative thoughts someone may have brought in. These Earth energies are beneficial and should be treated with respect. Therefore say a prayer of protection and be prepared to communicate with any spirits that may be attracted.

There is a healing side to geospirals. If you are feeling under the weather or recovering from a sickness or an operation spend 15 to 30 minutes sitting or lying in the circles of a geospiral. Your body will appreciate it.

If you have a loved one in hospital or in a bed at home, take a pillow or cushion to a geospiral, leave it basking in the energy for half an hour, then take it to the loved one's bedside. They will appreciate and benefit from the natural healing energy.

THE CREATIVE SIDE: Relaxing within the rings of a geospiral can trigger many creative thoughts. If you are looking for ideas keep this general thought in mind as you go to meditate at a geospiral. You may be surprised at the ideas that come forth. Keep a notebook and pencil handy and do not be afraid to make notes as an idea springs nimbly into your Conscious Mind. Do not wait until you get home because, like dreams, the idea will be gone. If you do get a great idea thank the Universe, your Creator, the Source of Your Being.

HOLY DIRT, SACRED EARTH: If you seek further information on geo-spirals and our dowsing studies in New Mexico find a copy of "Holy Dirt, Sacred Earth: A Dowser's Journey in New Mexico."

LOS LUNAS DOWSERS: Talking of New Mexico, some years back I had the honor of speaking and showing color pictures of our research in northern New Mexico to the monthly meeting of the Willow-benders, the Los Lunas Chapter of the American Society of Dowsers. Next day, Chairman Gary Plapp, myself and Betty Lou and a number of dedicated members, headed out for a Field Trip to check out the energies around a large display of petroglyphs, artworks in stone left by Indian Ancestors hundreds of years ago.

We quickly found a series of geospirals in the desert below the basalt rocks which indicated a strong Native Indian presence centuries ago. One interesting point there were two large blind springs but both were empty, yet the geospirals continued to manifest their energies. We wondered why?

One massive rock, we dowsed out to be ten tons, was positioned over a 21-ring geospiral. Five other geospirals close by indicated a vortex. We sat on the rock for at least fifteen minutes and everyone admitted they had no desire to get up and leave. Such is the power of the magnetic qualities of a geospiral.

As Betty Lou said afterwards: "It was a most memorable day sur-rounded by enthusiastic dowsers all trekking over sand dunes and scaling rocks."

THE LEYS OF OUR ANCESTORS

Planet Earth is laced with a strange and mysterious phenomenon called ley lines. To all intents and purposes they travel or are seen in straight lines even as they bend round the surface of the Earth.

To make matters worse there is no rhyme nor reason for them except they are extraordinarily useful to animals and humankind. Plus, once upon a time in ancient days they were used by our historic ancestors to move from one camp, one harbor, one sacred place to another. Leys were a natural tracking system. They knew that if they followed and stayed in tune with this particular line of energy it would take them to a distant destination point. Today we use GPS or Global Positioning System mainly because we do not like walking. Sitting in a traveling armchair (you might call it automobile) going at 70 mph is infinitely more attractive and less time consuming.

Still, what was good for native people was good for settlers so that many cities and towns in the world were built on leys. In fact a place where leys crossed saw the establishment of many cities such as Boston, New York, Philadelphia, Washington all are centers for multiple leys. Even smaller communities normally with universities and major colleges will often have up to four leys running through such as Princeton which actually has five. The fifth one runs through the Institute for Advanced Studies where Dr. Einstein hung his hat for two decades.

One strange phenomenon about leys is that they always run straight. So that in a universe where straight is odd is quite peculiar. Only humans appear to enjoy creating straight forms: check the tiles on the floor, the walls of rooms, the corridor, even paper is neatly cut into straight lines.

Some leys form single or double lines. Occasionally they manifest in three lines or hairs, in which case we refer to them as triple-haired leys. There is really no set length for leys. One might go hundreds of miles while another might run a mere mile. The only constant is they exist in straight lines, even when crossing water such as lakes, rivers and oceans. According to lunar movements they appear to intensify at full moon and again at new moon but these movements are minimal. In addition they have been found to move a few feet but they do return.

Some supposed gurus who have probably never stopped to enjoy time on a ley, have branded some of them negative which is far from the truth, in fact leys manifest Yin feminine energy and have wide areas of influence which is wonderful.

When Betty Lou and I checked the great North and South Broad Street ley that runs through a stack of hospitals, scientific research institutions, artistic academies and entertainment centers, dowsing showed an area of influence spanning about fifty yards on each side of the line.

A dowser once suggested that ley lines are being projected on the planet from outer space. No one appears to have come up with any further information.

In Modern ley history the phenomenon did not surface until 1921 when an English flour mill owner and avid photographer took notice. Alfred Watkins was riding his horse in Hertfordshire, a county north of London, when he noticed that many of the foot paths and lanes seemed to connect one hilltop to another in a straight line. He subsequently coined the term "ley" because the lines passed through places whose names contained the syllables "ley, lay, lea, lee, or leigh."

In an intensive study of maps he noticed that key points were in alignment. For instance, churches built on old pagan or Celtic spiritual sites appeared mysteriously in a line.

"The whole thing came to me in a flash," he later told his son. Watkins subsequently found ley lines that connected standing stones, ancient earthworks, stone monuments and circles, cairns, megaliths, barrows and sites of ancient towns and villages. In his book, Early British Trackways published in 1922, he describes his various findings.

The book triggered a new movement among archaeologists, hikers and of course dowsers. Suddenly historical events were shown in a new light. Leys were used by ancient Britons to move from one community to another. They sensed the energy or they followed the stone markers. Following Watkins's revelations British dowsers quickly found major leys in Glastonbury, Stonehenge, Avebury, St. Michael's Mount, and in major cities.

The interesting point about leys while they run straight across land and water, do not appear to be based on an association with water, and yet geospirals, which are water-based can often be found close to leys, particularly leys that cross.

Where the leys cross and are accompanied by geospirals, the Yin energy becomes so intense that it actually swirls, domes, and presents a phenomenon known as the vortex. These are places for healing, visions, dreams, creativity and simply hanging out. These can be found in various places of the world, notably Sedona (Arizona), Taos (New Mexico), Glastonbury, Stonehenge, Avebury (United Kingdom), Rome (Italy), Baalbek (Lebanon), the Great Pyramid at Giza, Luxor and Alexandria (Egypt) to name a few.

If only the archaeologists and various academics would get off their cultural and ritualistic "science thinking" and resort to developing their intuitive gifts such as radiesthesia, dowsing and divining, we might know of many more.

In my book Chasing the Cosmic Principle: Dowsing from Pyramids to Back Yard America the reader is taken along the progress of leys of ancient Egypt, the Middle East, Rome, Paris and London to the leys that lace around us in North America.

Since publication of the book, we discovered a major ley. As this section is on leys we thought you would be interested.

THE GREAT EAST CANADA—UNITED STATES CORRIDOR LEY PRINCE EDWARD ISLAND TO MOBILE, ALABAMA

Originally our research showed a ley line existing from Boston to Washington DC but further examination indicated it might be found further north-east in Prince Edward Island, Canada and further south-west in Mobile, Alabama. Length is about 1,700 miles or 2,700 kilometers.

The ley comes out of the Atlantic at Prince Edward Island and heads south-east through Charlottetown where it cuts through the center of St. Dunstan's Basilica, the Cathedral of the Catholic Diocese. Named after St. Dunstan, the Anglo-Saxon saint from Glastonbury, UK it is a splendid example of French Gothic architecture.

The ley is next found at Boston's Paul Revere Mall and the Freedom Trail before advancing south-west to Queens in New York City where it passes through Rainey Park, named after Dr. Thomas Rainey. The doctor spent most of his active life and fortune fighting for construction of an East River Bridge linking Manhattan and Long Island City. Plans collapsed during the financial panic of 1873. A baseball field now exists where one of the bridge supports would have been, a point where the ley exists. The ley continues on to Trenton, New Jersey where it passes through the NJ State Museum and Friends of New Jersey buildings by County Route 29.

After crossing the Delaware River, the ley is next found in Philadelphia, Pennsylvania where it passes through the Swann Memorial Fountain at Logan Square. Also known as the Fountain of the Three Rivers, the memorial is a fountain sculpture created by Alexander Stirling Calder with the complete memorial designed by architect Wilson Eyre. Opened in 1924 it was and still is a spectacular crowd pleaser and a big attraction for youngsters who delight in splashing through the water. Like most leys, there are geospirals in and around the area, therefore earth energies add to the attraction.

From Philadelphia the ley continues to Wilmington, Delaware where it passes through the Frederick Douglas Stubbs School and Kirkwood Park, then on to the Old Swedes Church. Found at 606 North Church Street it is the oldest church in the United States standing as originally built and still in use as a house of worship. Erected in 1698–1699 by descendents of the Swedish colonists who crossed the Atlantic aboard the Kalmar Nickel in 1638, it is a National Historic Site. The ley runs through the Church and crosses Lord Street.

From Delaware the East Corridor Ley goes to Baltimore, Maryland where it can be found among the scholars at the St. Paul's Education Department. It then runs on south-west to Washington, DC and crosses through the White House. If one stands on the Pennsylvania Avenue side of the General Lafayette Statue you will be on the East Corridor Ley.

The ley heads on south-west to Atlanta, Georgia where it passes through McDonough Field at Emerson University at Druid Hills. Continuing, the ley cuts through Mobile, Alabama and seekers will find it in the Plaza of the Cathedral of the Immaculate Conception. It was the first Catholic parish established in the early 1700s on the Gulf Coast

Now tell us that these cities and two cathedrals were built on a ley line by sheer coincidence and we will say "Foooey!"

COORDINATES FOR LEY HUNTERS
EAST CORRIDOR LEY
PEI, Canada. St. Dunstan's Cathedral. 46°14′01.10" N 63°07′57.09" W
Boston, Mass. Paul Revere Mall. 42°21′57.27" N 71°03′13.58" W
New York City, Rainey Park, Queens. 40°45′58.93" N 73°56′27.11" W

Trenton, NJ. State Museum 40°13′16.12" N 74°46′26.57" W

Philadelphia Pa. Swann Memorial 39°57′28.49" N 75°10′14.12" W

Wilmington, De. Old Swedes Church 39°44′16.88" N 75°32′30.15" W

Baltimore, Ma. St. Paul's Education Dept. 39°17′46.39" N 76°36′38.21" W

Washington, DC. The White House. 38°53′51.65" N 77°02′11.60" W

Atlanta, Ga. Emerson Univ. 33°47′40.12" N 84°19′29.18" W

Mobile, Al. Catholic Cathedral 30°41′25.36" N 88°02′42.20" W

15

TOMORROW: AN EARTH ENERGY UTOPIA?

In closing this note on Earth energy it seems important to visualize a time in the future. It is a time when folks who are creating families and finding safe homes are guaranteed the right atmosphere and environment for healthy, positive and safe living.

The day has to come when Official America embracing Washington D.C., plus local government along with all the industries that should be responsible for these beneficial qualities — lawyers, realtors, construction, developers, — recognize there is a silent killer known as geopathic stress lurking in homes, offices, farms and community places and install safeguards — even on highways.

Among all the legal jargon on paper that goes towards the sale, leasing or rental of a property will be a little box waiting for a check mark against the words: This building is hereby certified permanently free of any toxic energy, notably geopathic stress."

Or as we dowsers have termed it: "The Silent Killer Below."

SOURCES THAT MAY HELP

BOOKS ON DOWSING AND EARTH ENERGIES

Earth Radiation by Käthe Bachler & John Living

Pendulum Power by Greg Neilsen

The Patterns of the Past by Guy Underwood

Effects of Harmful Radiations & Noxious Rays by American Society of Dowsers 1974

Geopathic Zones & the Iron Stake Method by Gregory Storozuk

Letter To Robin: A Mini Course In Pendulum Dowsing by Walter Woods

Healing Sick Houses, Dowsing for Healthy Homes, by Roy and Ann Proctor

The Diviner's Handbook by Tom Graves

The Essential Dowsing Guide by Dennis Wheatley

Aquavideo, an instruction guide by Bill Cox

Dowsing for Health by Arthur Bailey

The Ley Hunters Companion by Paul Devereux & Ian Thomson

It's a Whole New World by Jeff Jeffries

American Society of Dowsers, The Water Dowsers Manual, compiled by Maria Perry

Earthing by Clinto Ober, Stephen Sinatra & Martin Zucker

Cancer: The full menu by Rolf Gordon

On Physics of Geopathogenic Phenomena by Joesph A Kopp (Research Paper in ASD Publication)

Effects of Harmful Radiations & Noxious Rays, ASD Publication 1974.

HOLY DIRT, SACRED EARTH: A Dowser's Journey in New Mexico by Robert Egby (geospirals)

Chasing the Cosmic Principle: Dowsing from Pyramids to Back Yard America by Robert Egby

VIDEOS AND LINKS

American Society of Dowsers Bookstore
http://www.dowsers.org/

The Canadian Society of Dowsers
http://canadiandowsers.org/

The British Society of Dowsers
https://britishdowsers.org/

The Canadian Society of Questers, Vancouver BC
https://questers.ca/#

G.S a common factor in most illnesses by Rolf Gordon
https://dulwichhealth.co.uk/geopathic-stress-by-rolf-gordon/

G.S. explained by Canadian dowser Susan Collins
https://www.youtube.com/watch?v=dh8uMWdOdQo

G.S. & Pavement Distress in India
http://www.iosrjournals.org/iosr-jmce/papers/sicete(civil)-volume4/37.pdf

Savitribai Phule Pune University, India
http://www.unipune.ac.in/

Geopathic Stress in India
https://www.researchgate.net/profile/Nandkumar_Dharmadhikari

Geopathic Stress cleared remotely — Jeff Jeffries
https://www.intelligentenergies.com/

Helios 3: Geopathic Stress harmonizer
http://www.helios3.com/

Australian Dowsers of NSW
http://www.dowsingaustralia.com/

CPSIA information can be obtained
at www.ICGtesting.com
Printed in the USA
BVHW070259160122
626297BV00004B/275